EVALUATING VIEWPOINTS:
CRITICAL THINKING IN
UNITED STATES HISTORY SERIES

TEACHER'S GUIDE

BOOK TWO
NEW REPUBLIC
TO
CIVIL WAR

KEVIN O'REILLY

SERIES TITLES:
BOOK 1–COLONIES TO CONSTITUTION
BOOK 2–NEW REPUBLIC TO CIVIL WAR
BOOK 3–RECONSTRUCTION TO PROGRESSIVISM
BOOK 4–SPANISH-AMERICAN WAR TO VIETNAM WAR

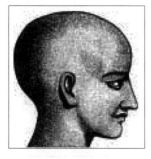

© 1984, 1993
CRITICAL THINKING BOOKS & SOFTWARE
www.criticalthinking.com
P.O. Box 448 • Pacific Grove • CA 93950-0448
Phone 800-458-4849 • FAX 831-393-3277
ISBN 0-89455-416-6
Printed in the United States of America

TABLE OF CONTENTS

ABOUT THE AUTHOR

Kevin O'Reilly is a social studies teacher at Hamilton-Wenham Regional High School in Massachusetts. He was named by *Time* magazine and the National Council for the Social Studies as the 1986 Outstanding Social Studies Teacher in the United States. In addition to these four volumes on Critical Thinking in Unites States History, Mr. O'Reilly is the coauthor of *Critical Viewing: Stimulant to Critical Thinking* (also published by Critical Thinking Press & Software, formerly Midwest Publications), and the author of "Escalation," a computer simulation on the Vietnam War (Kevin O'Reilly, 6 Mason Street, Beverly, MA 01915). Mr. O'Reilly, who has a Master of Arts Degree in History, is an editor of the *New England Journal of History*. He conducts workshops throughout the United States on critical thinking, critical viewing, and decision-making.

FOR
Lynn
with all my love

ACKNOWLEDGMENTS

I would like to thank the following for their help: the Schlesinger Library staff for its help in researching women's history both in a summer institute and for Lesson 7 of this book; Old Sturbridge Village for permission to use "A Farm Woman's Diary" and "Accounts: The Davis Family" and the Baker Library at Harvard University as well for the Davis Family (Lesson 6); the Library of Congress, especially Maja Keech who supplied valuable information about slavery visuals, and the National Archives for locating the pictures for Lesson 17; my wife, who has supported me through this project, which has lasted now for 13 years from the beginning of writing the first version of Book 1 to this completion of the revised edition of Book 2.

INTRODUCTION

Overview of This Section

This teacher's guide contains an introduction; reproducible introductory lessons for each skill covered in the series; suggested teaching strategies and answers for each lesson in the student text; and test questions. The introduction includes

1. an introduction to the process of critical thinking;

2. a rationale for the series;

3. a description of the role of the teacher, including an overview of the *Teacher's Guide*, suggestions for classroom methods for teaching critical thinking in history, and various suggestions for evaluating student progress;

4. a description of the role of the student, including an overview of the student text;

5. a chart of the scope and sequence of skills developed in this text;

6. a bibliography of sources on critical thinking.

What Is Critical Thinking?

One author calls critical thinking "reasoned judgment." For the purposes of this series, critical thinking is *judging* the worth of claims or arguments. It involves judgment, assessment, and evaluation. The critical thinker has a healthy skepticism and asks probing questions; the noncritical thinker is likely to jump to conclusions and believe whatever is claimed.

Critical thinking is not the same as creative thinking, brainstorming, problem solving, decision making, conceptualizing, or Bloom's taxonomy—although it is involved in the judgment phase of problem solving and decision making. Neither is it the same as asking students to compare and contrast or to categorize—for those activities do not require students to evaluate the comparisons made or categories delineated.

Only level six (evaluation) of Bloom's taxonomy involves critical thinking. Level four (analysis) is so important to evaluation of arguments, however, that some of these skills are also directly taught in these books.

The following analysis and evaluation skills are included in the series.

©1993 Critical Thinking Press & Software, P.O. Box 448, Pacific Grove, CA 93950 (800) 458-4849

> ### — Analysis Skills —
>
> * Differentiating between conclusions and reasons
>
> * Identifying types of reasoning
>
> * Identifying sources of information
>
> * Classifying parts of an argument based on cue words, value words, emotional words, and change-of-direction words
>
> * Identifying assumptions and value judgments
>
> ### — Evaluation Skills —
>
> * Evaluating the relevance of reasons to conclusions
>
> * Evaluating types of reasoning
>
> * Evaluating sources
>
> * Evaluating assumptions and value judgments

Overall, then, the critical thinker asks, "Why should I believe this?" and offers reasoned judgments in answer to that question. These books are meant to arm students with the critical-thinking skills necessary to make reasoned judgments, to prod them into asking questions, and to give them the confidence both to ask questions and to offer judgments.

About This Series

This four-volume series, Evaluating Viewpoints: Critical Thinking in United States History, is intended to improve critical thinking through evaluation of conflicting viewpoints of United States history. The books are chronological, each covering a particular time period.

*Book 1: Colonies to Constitution
    (1492–1789)*

*Book 2: New Republic to Civil War
    (1790–1865)*

*Book 3: Reconstruction to Progressivism
    (1865–1914)*

*Book 4: Spanish-American War to Vietnam War
    (1900–1980)*

There is not, however, chronological coverage within each book. Each lesson is a self-contained problem that can be "plugged in" at any point in a corresponding history unit. These books are thus meant to supplement other curriculum materials, not to be the sole text for a course.

As mentioned in the introduction of the student text, the root word of history is *story*. In this series, emphasis is on helping students see that the "story" of history can be told in different ways and that values, attitudes, perceptions, and selection all shape the way people see the past. These books are intended to show students that historical subject matter is not some unchanging, agreed upon, and complete subject to be memorized, but rather is changing, selective, fragmentary, and open to interpretation.

The target of this series is understanding, not memorizing. Studies in cognitive psychology indicate that memorization lasts only a short time. Focusing on problems, thinking, and understanding helps students remember the content of history much longer.

The Role of the Teacher

About the Teacher's Guide

The *Teacher's Guide* contains
1. an introduction to the series;
2. reproducible worksheets for introducing each skill;
3. objectives, teaching ideas, and suggested answers for each lesson;
4. possible test questions and suggested answers.

Twelve skill worksheets are included in the *Teacher's Guide* of each book in the series. These can be used to promote a questioning attitude (Worksheet A), introduce particular skills (Worksheets B–J), or serve as general worksheets for evaluating any film or written argument (Worksheets K–L). The teaching ideas and the suggested answers are intended as guidance for the teacher, not as rigid lesson plans or right answers. The emphasis is on thinking, not on "correct" answers.

A key element in the emphasis on teaching, practicing, and repeating critical thinking skills is the "Scope and Sequence of Skills" chart on pages 12–13. Once you have decided which skills to teach, this chart will serve as a quick reference to their location in each book and to help you select appropriate lessons for practice and repetition. Values are included under "Assumptions" in the scope-and-sequence chart, since they are a kind of assumption about the way the world should be. Those lessons focusing on values are marked with a "v."

Some skills are not represented on the scope-and-sequence chart. Although these skills are not **explicitly** taught in any lesson in the book, they are a part of many of the problem lessons. For example, finding the main idea is an important part of evaluating the interpretations in the book. The importance of using key words for encoding parts of arguments is also a part of many problem lessons, but is never explicitly taught in any specific lesson. For further information on critical thinking, refer to the Bibliography of Sources on Critical Thinking on page 11 in this book.

Classroom Methods for Teaching Critical Thinking in History

Unlike other anthologies of opposing viewpoints, this series focuses on how to analyze and evaluate arguments. In improving athletic performance, coaches know that a systematic approach works best. Skills must be broken down and their components explained; the athlete has to try the skill with the guidance of the coach; the athlete must repeatedly practice the skill; and, finally, the skills must be applied in the athletic contest. This same method is used in these books to teach skills of critical thinking. Each skill is broken down and explained in the "Guide to Critical Thinking"; with the guidance of the teacher and/ or other students, the student tries the skill on worksheets; additional worksheets provide practice as the student repeats the skill; and, finally, the student applies the skill to new opposing-viewpoint problems. This pattern of skill instruction is outlined below.

Pattern of Skill Instruction

1. INITIAL PROBLEM

In the books in this series, students are confronted with a historical problem from the student text. Since the problem consists of opposing viewpoints, students are forced to evaluate the viewpoints to arrive at a conclusion. This raises the need to learn to think critically in deciding which viewpoint to believe.

2. FAMILIAR EXAMPLE

The teacher gives the class an everyday problem, either from the "Guide to Critical Thinking" or an introductory worksheet, on the skill involved in step 1. Familiar examples make it easier for students to learn the skill.

3. METACOGNITION

This step offers direct teaching of analysis and/or evaluation skills. As the class discusses answers to the familiar problem in step 2, they discuss how class members arrived at their answers. The focus here is on *metacognition*—thinking about thinking, not about the content of the problem—and the components are taught directly. What is involved in performing the skill? What are the steps in the skill? What are the criteria for evaluation? A diagram of the steps or criteria is then posted in the classroom and/or drawn in the "skills" section of students' notebooks. Ideally, the students, guided by the teacher, will identify the components of the skill; those the class cannot identify can be taught directly by the teacher using the "Guide to Critical Thinking."

4.	GUIDED PRACTICE	The students are referred back to the historical problem in step 1 and directed to discuss its evaluation in light of the skill they have learned. The students employ the skill on the problem and on worksheets with the guidance of the teacher and other students.
5.	MASTERY	Students repeatedly practice the skill on additional worksheets and in class discussions.
6.	EXTENSION	As the course progresses, students extend the skill as they apply it to new historical problems.

Class Discussions

From this emphasis on specific critical thinking skills, it can be seen that class discussions of the opposing viewpoints presented in the books are not to be free-for-alls, where all opinions are equally good. Students are expected to employ the skills learned in previous classes, to question assertions made by their classmates, and to defend their own assertions with evidence and reasons. This is a far cry from an emphasis on right answers. In this series, the emphasis is on good thinking, not on right answers.

Adaptation

Obviously, some of the lessons in this text are more difficult than others. Teachers can make easy lessons more challenging by eliminating step-by-step questions or worksheets or by making students produce their own examples to illustrate particular skills. Lessons that are too difficult for some classes can be made easier by doing only a portion of the lesson, by focusing on only a single skill, or by giving students the step-by-step worksheet on the topic. Refer to teaching suggestions on specific lessons for further guidance in the difficulty level of each lesson within this book.

Using the "Guide to Critical Thinking"

The "Guide to Critical Thinking," the first unit in each student text, is meant to help teachers with the direct instruction of key elements of the various critical thinking skills. These key skills are summarized in the chart on pages 12–13.

Although the Guide touches on numerous skills related to the evaluation of interpretations or arguments, it focuses on four of these skills: evaluation of evidence, evaluation of cause-and-effect reasoning, evaluation of comparison reasoning (analogy), and evaluation of generalizations. A grasp of these four argument components is an enormous help in the students' ability to think critically.

The section on *evidence* emphasizes the idea of sources of information. Rather than distinguishing between evidence, which has a source, and information, which provides no source, students are simply instructed to ask, "Is there a source?" whenever they encounter information in support of a claim. If not, they are to note that weakness. If yes, they are to evaluate it. Introductory Worksheet B (pp. 33–34 in this book) provides a concrete problem for determining and evaluating evidence.

In the section on *reasoning*, it is again important to note that students are not only taught to identify the type of reasoning but also to evaluate it. It is not enough that a student says, "This is a cause-and-effect argument." The student must also say whether it is a strong or weak cause-and-effect argument and give reasons for saying so. A concrete problem for introducing cause-and-effect reasoning can be found in the teaching ideas for Introductory Worksheet E (pp. 39–40 in this book).

The section on *evaluating comparisons* (analogies) is not the same as the activity of compare and contrast. This critical thinking skill focuses on evaluating comparison arguments, or what is sometimes called analogic reasoning. For example, asking students to compare and contrast the fighting in Nicaragua in the 1980s with the Vietnam War is very different from asking them to evaluate the argument "The United States should not be involved in fighting in Nicaragua because it will turn into another Vietnam." Although both assignments involve basic knowledge of the two situations, the second assignment requires students to identify the type of reasoning used and to implement comparison and contrast without being cued to do so (as in the first assignment). A concrete problem for introducing comparison reasoning is in the teaching ideas for Introductory Worksheet F (pp. 41–42 in this book).

The term *generalization*, rather than *sample reasoning*, is used for this skill. Use the pizza example on page 8 of the student book as a concrete problem for introducing generalizations. Ask, "Suppose you bit into a pizza and the bite was cold. What might you conclude about the pizza?" The strength of a generalization can be determined by asking, "How large and representative is the sample?" Some people, however, believe that randomness is better than representativeness as a method for achieving an accurate sample. In any event, you might want to mention to your students that randomness is also a commonly accepted method of sampling.

Fallacies, although included with each type of reasoning, are not emphasized either in the Guide or in the lessons. Simply teaching students a few questions to ask (and the willingness to ask them) within several broad areas of reasoning will usually be more helpful than teaching them a larger number of fallacies and having them try to fit real arguments into one of these fallacies.

Several points emphasized in the ARMEAR model on page 18 in the student text are not emphasized elsewhere in the Guide. One such point is questions about the author (A); the second is relevant information (R). Students should be taught to bring any information that might be relevant to bear on the topic. They may, of course, have difficulty determining what is relevant. Additionally, they are not in the habit of seeing the relevance of one topic to another. To encourage the habit of thinking about what might be relevant to a historical problem, a number of lessons include relevant information sheets. Students who don't use the sheets can't do a complete analysis of the arguments. Encouraging this habit of calling on what they know helps students view history as a fund of knowledge to be drawn upon to help provide perspective on other, similar issues. History thereby becomes more meaningful.

Skill Transfer

Many of the worksheets contain both everyday and historic argument examples. This mixture is intended to promote transfer of the skills learned into other areas of the students' lives. Teachers can facilitate this transfer of critical thinking skills learned in history class to other subject areas by having students debate topics then analyze the reasoning they used in the debate. When students realize that they use the same reasoning elements in their own thinking, they are more likely to transfer them into other areas of their lives. Another important method for promoting skill transfer is to listen carefully to student chatter before class starts. If you can ask a question on the use of a particular type of reasoning on a topic heard in a student conversation, you will connect the skill learned in history to the students' everyday lives.

Evaluation

Test questions are provided at the end of this teacher's guide, and the many problem sheets in the student text provide even more possible test questions. Of course, teachers should consider the viewpoints in the longer problems for essay assignments. These can be evaluation essays, such as "Evaluate Historian A's argument on immigration. In your essay identify and evaluate two pieces of evidence and two types of reasoning."

WRITING AND THINKING

Writing skills are an important part of this curriculum, and students should be held accountable for their critical thinking skills when they write any essay assignment. A sample student assignment might be, "Write a minimum 250-word essay on the main cause of the Civil War. In your essay you are to show what makes a strong cause, support your case with one piece of evidence, and explain why this is strong evidence." Students must learn how to construct strong arguments in addition to evaluating the arguments made by others.

Overview of Book 2

Book 2 is comprised of the "Guide to Critical Thinking" (Unit 1), ten introductory lessons, and twenty-seven lessons divided into three units. Lessons 1–9 are in the New Republic Unit; Lessons 10–18 in the Slavery Unit; Lessons 19–27 in the Civil War Unit. The table of contents and the scope-and-sequence chart show the specific topic and the emphasized skills of each lesson.

> Lessons with titles phrased as questions are historical problems, rather than worksheets. These problems involve numerous skills and focus on historical issues; worksheets focus on a specific skill and mix everyday, modern examples with historical content.

The first four skills in the scope-and-sequence chart (evidence, cause and effect, comparison, and generalization) involve both identification and evaluation. A few lessons focus on just identification or evaluation, but most consider both. Values are included under assumptions in the scope-and-sequence chart since values are assumptions about the way the world should be.

Some skills are not represented in the scope-and-sequence chart as they are not explicitly taught in any of the lessons. They are a part of the historical-problem lessons, however. Finding the main idea and using key words for encoding parts of arguments are two such skills.

Some teachers will prefer to use just the historical-problem lessons (Lessons 6–9, 14–18, and 23–27). These problem lessons can be used to teach a variety of skills and are interesting topics to study. Worksheet lessons, on the other hand, provide practice in particular skills which help students do more complete analyses of the interpretations in the problem lessons. The worksheet lessons provide sequencing of each skill.

The list of major sources used (pp. 189–93 in the student text) shows that the viewpoints in Book 2 are based on the views of major historians: Glenda Riley and Sara Evans on Women's Rights; Stanley Elkins, Robert Fogel, Stanley Engerman, John Blassingame on slavery; Charles Beard, James Randall, and Bruce Catton on the Civil War.

While these are all well known interpretations, some are highly controversial. People may argue that some of the interpretations are quite fanciful, not credible enough to bring to student's attention. But if the interpretations are weak, let the students recognize their weaknesses. Good arguments are judged good because they are stronger than bad arguments. Students need to encounter and evaluate both. Because of this need for student judgment, there are no standard right and wrong answers to the problems in this book.

The Role of the Student

The student book contains the "Guide to Critical Thinking" and twenty-seven lessons involving critical thinking. The "Guide to Critical Thinking" is intended to be used when students have a need to learn the components of a particular skill. While some may find it worthwhile to read through the whole Guide to get an overview of the skills involved in argument evaluation, it is not recommended that students study all the various skills at once. Rather, they should refer to the part of the Guide that explains the skill they are currently learning.

The historical lessons consist of both a short problem section for practicing skills (1–2 pages each) and longer historical problems (2–27 pages each) with opposing viewpoints. Paragraphs in longer viewpoints are numbered to make discussion and referencing easier.

Particular skills, especially generalizations and cause-and-effect reasoning, are explained with visual models. These have proven helpful for many students, some of whom regularly use them to help evaluate arguments on tests.

These books focus on formulating good arguments as well as evaluating arguments offered by others. In this way, students should begin to question their own assumptions, points of view, and prejudices. This self-criticism, referred to by Richard Paul as "critical thinking in the strong sense," is an important, if difficult, goal to achieve.

Students should begin to see historical knowledge as changing, selective, fragmentary, and open to question. This change in student attitudes about the nature of historical knowledge (epistemology) is as important as their mastery of critical thinking skills. Beginning with Worksheet A, students should be encouraged, even expected, to question viewpoints presented. The problem format helps students see history the way it really is and to ask questions. It also makes history much more interesting.

Bibliography of Sources on Critical Thinking

Beyer, Barry. *Practical Strategies for the Teaching of Thinking.* Boston: Allyn and Bacon, 1987.

———— "Teaching Critical Thinking: A Direct Approach." *Social Education* 49 (April 1985): 297–303.

Bloch, Marc. *The Historian's Craft.* New York: Random House, 1953.

Bloom, Benjamin S., ed. *Taxonomy of Educational Objectives, Handbook I: Cognitive Domain.* New York: David McKay, 1956.

Carr, Edward Harlett. *What Is History?* New York: Random House, 1961.

Copi, Irving. *Introduction to Logic.* 5th ed. New York: Macmillan, 1978.

Costa, Arthur. "Teaching For, Of, and About Thinking." In *Developing Minds: A Resource Book for Teaching Thinking.* Edited by Arthur L. Costa, 20–24. Alexandria, VA: Association for Supervision and Curriculum Development, 1985.

Costa, Arthur and Lawrence Lowery. *Techniques for Teaching Thinking.* Pacific Grove, CA: Critical Thinking Press, 1989.

Crossley, David J., and Peter Wilson. *How to Argue.* New York: Random House, 1979.

Fisher, David Hackett. *Historians' Fallacies: Toward a Logic of Historical Thought.* New York: Harper and Row, 1970.

Gustavson, Carl. *A Preface to History.* New York: McGraw-Hill, 1955.

Norris, Stephen. "The Reliability of Observation Statements." *Rational Thinking Reports,* No. 4. Urbana, IL: University of Illinois, 1979.

Norris, Stephen and Robert Ennis. *Evaluating Critical Thinking.* Pacific Grove, CA: Critical Thinking Press, 1989.

O'Reilly, Kevin. "Teaching Critical Thinking in High School U.S. History." *Social Education* 49 (April 1985): 281–4.

———— "Vietnam: A Case Study for Critical Thinking" (videotape). Pleasantville, NY: Educational Audiovisual, 1989.

Paul, Richard. "Critical Thinking: Fundamental to Education for a Free Society." *Educational Leadership* 42 (September 1984): 4–14.

Roden, Philip. *The Elusive Truth.* Glenview, IL: Scott-Foresman, 1973.

Sanders, Norris. *Classroom Questions: What Kinds?* New York: Harper and Row, 1966.

Swartz, Robert and D. N. Perkins. *Teaching Thinking: Issues and Approaches.* Pacific Grove, CA: Critical Thinking Press, 1989.

Weddle, Perry. *Argument: A Guide to Critical Thinking.* New York: McGraw-Hill, 1977.

Scope and Sequence of Skills • Book 2

Abbreviations used in this chart are as follows: **(TG)**–Teacher's Guide; **(GTC)**–"Guide to Critical Thinking," Unit 1 in Student Book; **(d)**–Debating reasoning; **(e)**–Eliminating alternatives; **(f)**–Frame of reference; **(v)**–Values.

Lesson	Topic	Evidence	Cause/Effect	Comparison	Generalization	Assumption	Relevant Information	Proof and Debating
Concrete Example		TG 14	TG 19	TG 39	GCT 8	–	–	–
Explanation		GCT 2	GCT 5	GCT 7	GCT 8	GCT 15	GCT 18	GCT 11

Introductory Worksheets

Lesson	Topic	Evidence	Cause/Effect	Comparison	Generalization	Assumption	Relevant Information	Proof and Debating
A	Bermuda Triangle	▨	▨		▨	▨		
B, C, D	Evaluating Evidence	▨						
E	Cause and Effect Reasoning		▨					
F, G	Evaluating Comparisons			▨				
H	Evaluating Generalizations				▨			
I, J	Identifying Assumptions					▨		

New Republic

Lesson	Topic	Evidence	Cause/Effect	Comparison	Generalization	Assumption	Relevant Information	Proof and Debating
1	New Republic	▨						
2	New Republic	▨						
3	New Republic		▨					
4	Westward Expansion	▨	▨					
5	New Republic			▨				
6	Early Industrialization	▨	▨		▨			
7	Perceptions of Women	▨			▨			
8	Women's Rights	▨			▨	▨ (v)		
9	Andrew Jackson	▨			▨	▨		▨ (d)

Scope and Sequence of Skills • Book 2 (continued)

Slavery

Lesson	Topic	Evidence	Cause/Effect	Comparison	Generalization	Assumption	Relevant Information	Proof and Debating
10	Slavery	■						
11	Slave Resistance and Abolitionism		■					
12	Slave Work and Families				■			
13	Slavery		■	■				
14	Slavery	■			■			
15	Slave Conditions	■	■	■	■		■	
16	Slave Conditions	■	■	■	■	■	■	
17	Slavery	■	■		■			
18	Slave Diet	■	■		■		■	■ (e)

Civil War

Lesson	Topic	Evidence	Cause/Effect	Comparison	Generalization	Assumption	Relevant Information	Proof and Debating
19	Causes of Civil War	■	■	■				
20	Kansas-Nebraska Act		■					
21	Causes of Civil War		■	■	■			
22	Civil War							■
23	Fort Sumter		■					■ (f)
24	Causes of Civil War	■	■	■		■		
25	Causes of Civil War		■		■	■		■
26	Emancipation Proclamation and England's Neutrality		■		■		■	
27	Racism against Blacks	■	■			■		

UNIT 1
INTRODUCTORY LESSONS FOR SKILL DEVELOPMENT

Worksheet A: The Bermuda Triangle

Objectives

To increase skepticism of what is read, seen, or heard
To develop inclination and ability to question statements

Teaching Ideas
PREPARATION

Give students copies of the first page of the worksheet (page 31) and ask them to write their reaction to it. Do not allow discussion at this point. Check to make sure everyone has written something. If some students say they don't understand what to write, tell them to write down how they feel about the reading, but don't go into any more detail. The whole idea is to avoid letting them know what reactions you are looking for.

USING THE WORKSHEET

Some students will accept the argument in the handout without any criticisms. Many students feel that anything written down must be true. When the discussion begins they will see that some of their classmates were more skeptical and that the argument should not have been blindly accepted.

When you distribute copies of the Relevant Information sheet (page 32), this lesson in skepticism should be reinforced. After students read the relevant information, the author's argument should look very weak.

EXTENDING THE LESSON

This reading might also be used to teach a number of other skills, such as finding the main idea, identifying value and emotional words, identifying assumptions and fallacies, and evaluating evidence.

Suggested Analysis

The author argues that one hundred ships go down each year, but does not compare that to the number of ships in the area (ten thousand distress calls) or to the number of sinkings in other areas of the ocean.

In paragraph 6 the author uses the "leading question technique" when he asks why pilot Cosner did not go on Flight 19. Maybe Cosner was constipated or had the flu. The later suggestion that he had a "peculiar feeling" is not really argued or supported by evidence. Similarly, the author suggests that the Navy is covering up the situation by not saying anything about it. But maybe the Navy has not bothered to deny it because the whole theory is so ridiculous.

Worksheet B: Evaluating Evidence

Objectives

To increase ability in identifying evidence
To increase ability in evaluating evidence

Teaching Ideas

INTRODUCING THE SKILL

To introduce the skills of identifying and evaluating evidence, take five students into the hallway, out of the class's sight, and tell them they are going to role-play a murder. Have three students stay near your classroom door, one student go 25 feet down the hall in one direction, and the other student go 25 feet in the opposite direction. Tell them they are to watch carefully. Hand one of the three students by the door a pen and tell him or her to point it at one of the other students in the hall and yell, "Bang!" Tell the "murdered" student to fall down.

Bring the five students back together, and tell them the rest of the class is going to ask them questions to figure out who committed the crime. Only the murderer may lie; the witnesses (everyone else in the hall) must tell the truth. Tell the other witnesses they must tell everything they know. They are not to hide information or try to confuse the class.

When using this in class, substitute the corresponding student name for each of the roles in italics.

Re-enter the classroom with the five students. Tell the class that *the victim* was just killed, and have that person sit down. Tell the class that their task is to figure out who did it by questioning the four witnesses. [At some point a student may ask where the murder weapon is. If so, produce the pen (tell them it's a poison-dart gun) and ask if they have any questions about the weapon. If they ask about fingerprints, say that only *the murderer's* fingerprints are on it.] Later, tell the class that you have a letter, dated a month ago, written by *the murderer* to a close friend saying he or she was going to get even with *the victim*. Don't be discouraged if the students don't ask very good questions. Even advanced classes have had difficulty with this introductory exercise.

After ten to fifteen minutes, tell the class that you're going to stop talking about who committed the murder and, instead, talk about the skill involved in trying to decide who did it. This is the metacognitive stage. Ask the class what they think evidence is. [Based on this activity: statements by witnesses, objects that were part of the event, or written documents.]

The best way to get at the criteria for evaluating evidence is to ask the general question: How did you decide which evidence to believe? This way the class will generate the criteria themselves. If the general question proves too difficult you can ask more specific questions:

Ask the class why they didn't believe *the murderer* when s/he said s/he didn't do it. [S/he had a reason to lie to protect him- or herself.] Suppose *the murderer* said *a witness* did it, and *that witness* said *the murderer* did it, and that's all the class knew. Could they have told who was guilty? [No.] So why did they believe *that witness* over *the murderer*? [Because other witnesses supported *that witness's* version by saying *the murderer* did it.] Suppose a third witness was around the corner when the murder occurred. Would that strengthen or weaken his/her evidence? [Weaken it.] Why? [The testimony is now given by someone who did not see the crime—a secondary source.] Is *the murderer* more likely to tell the truth in the trial or in a letter to a friend? [This is tricky, but the private letter is generally more reliable.]

REVIEWING THE SKILL

Write the criteria for evaluating evidence (see the section on **Evaluation** in the "Guide to Critical Thinking," student text, page 3) on the board and have students copy it into their notebooks. You could also ask a volunteer to make a poster to remind students of the criteria (below).

EVALUATING EVIDENCE

Is there a source for the information?

If no, the information is unsupported and weakened.

If yes, evaluate it:

    P — primary or secondary?

    R — reason to lie or exaggerate?

    O — other evidence to verify this evidence?

    P — public or private?

This process of making posters for the classroom can be repeated for other skills and their criteria.

USING THE WORKSHEET

When the class has completed the role-play activity and the discussion, you can pass out Worksheet B (pp. 33–34) as an immediate follow-up on evaluating evidence. Tell the students they are going to practice what they have just learned about evaluating evidence.

Suggested Answers

- The jury was probably right in its guilty verdict.

Point out that making the historical judgment that Lucky stabbed John Jones is not the same as finding him guilty in court. In history, unlike in court, we do not have to prove something "beyond a reasonable doubt," but rather provide enough evidence to show that the person probably did it. In other words, we might say we think Lucky committed the murder, but should have been found "not guilty" in court. We do not presume innocence in history as we do in trials.

A. Statements are numbers 1–10, 12, and 15–17.

B. Documents are numbers 14 and 18.

C. Objects are numbers 11 and 13.

- The evidence is evaluated as follows.

    P—Is the evidence primary?

    R—Does the person have a reason to lie?

    O—Is there other supporting evidence?

    P—Is the evidence private?

	4	7	10	11	14	17	18
P	no	yes	yes	yes	yes	no	no
R	yes	yes	no	no	no	no	no
O	no	yes	yes	yes	yes	yes	yes
P	no	no	no	yes	yes	yes	yes

- Since evidence 18 is private and seems to have no reason to lie, it is more reliable than evidence 4. Not foolproof; just more likely to be reliable.

Worksheet C: Sources and Evidence

Objectives

To identify sources
To evaluate evidence

Teaching Ideas
Using the Worksheet

Students must first determine if a source for the information is given. Then, if there is a source, they are to evaluate it according to the four questions explained in the Worksheet C handout.

Distribute copies of the worksheet and ask the students to complete as much as they can. Remind them that a longer explanation of evidence can be found on pages 2–4 in Unit 1 of their book.

When students have filled in as much of the sheet as they can, have them compare answers in groups of three. Finally, discuss the worksheet as a class.

Suggested Answers

1. Since the statement gives no source for the information, it cannot be further evaluated. Thus, the evidence is not well supported.

    [You will need to point out to some students that even though a specific figure ($15 million) is used, we do not know where the figure came from; no source is given.]

2. The scorebook is the source for the statistic. **P**—it is a primary source, since the scorekeeper had to be at the games; **R**—there is no reason for the scorebook (or scorekeeper) to lie about hits and times at bat (batting average); **O**—there is no other evidence given to support the claim that Kurt is a great hitter; **P**—it is a public statement. **Overall**, this would be considered a reliable source.

3. The three workers' statements at the public hearings are the source. **P**—the workers say they saw payoffs, so they are primary sources; **R**—the workers might have motives to lie or exaggerate if they do not like Mayor Pratt; **O**—the three workers verify each other; **P**—these are public statements. **Overall**, the fact that three people were willing to risk testifying about the corruption does carry some weight, although the evidence is not as reliable as that in problem 2.

4. There is no source given for the information, so it is not well supported.

Worksheet D: Evaluating Evidence — PROP

Objectives

To evaluate sources of evidence

Teaching Ideas
USING THE WORKSHEET

Pass out the worksheet. Ask the students to fill it in then discuss their answers as a class. If students are confused about any of the criteria, the following questions may help them clarify their evaluations.

QUESTIONS FOR DETERMINING EVIDENCE

- To determine if someone is **a primary source**, ask, "Was this person at the location when the event occurred, or was she talking about herself?"

- To determine if someone has **a reason to lie**, ask, "Did this person make him- or herself look good by the statement?" [Why would s/he lie to make him or herself look bad?]

- To determine if there is **other supporting evidence**, ask, "Who said this? Did any other people say the same thing?"

- To determine if the evidence is **public**, ask, "Did this person make the statement to influence anyone else? Does he or she think anyone other than the person spoken to would hear what was said?"

Suggested Answers

1. Yu-chi **P**—is a primary source; **R**—has a reason to lie; **O**—presents no supporting evidence; **P**—the statement is public, meant to influence his father. **Overall**, the evidence is not very reliable because of the reason to lie and the lack of supporting evidence.

2. Laura **P**—is a primary source about talking with Jill (but she was not at the scene of the baby-sitting); **R**—may have a reason to lie if she wants to protect Jill (we don't know); **O**—has supporting evidence provided by Connie's and Ellen's statements; **P**—the statement is public, meant to influence Bob. **Overall**, this is fairly good evidence.

3. Christie **P**—is a primary source; **R**—has no reason to lie, as her statement places the blame on herself; **O**—offers no supporting evidence; **P**—it is a public statement. **Overall**, Christie's evidence is strong. [Admitting she had done wrong is unlikely to be a lie, but it is possible—for example, if she had failed because she had skipped school, which might have gotten her into worse trouble.]

Worksheet E: Cause-and-Effect Reasoning

Objectives

To recognize cause-and-effect reasoning
To evaluate cause-and-effect reasoning

Teaching Ideas
INTRODUCING THE SKILL

Introduce cause-and-effect reasoning by telling the class that you, the teacher, just entered the emergency room with a terrible pain in your stomach. They are the doctors on duty. What would they ask? Set it up that you have been at the beach all day and left your ham and mayonnaise sandwich out in the hot sun.

Although some student may focus on what you ate and the likelihood of food poisoning early in the discussion, other students may later ask questions about appendicitis, medication, and alcohol. They are considering other possible causes for the problem. You could ask the class how they could test their hypothesis further to focus them on the connection between each proposed cause and effect. How could they check to be more certain it was food poisoning from the sandwich? (A blood test showing bacteria in the blood would show a connection).

REINFORCING THE SKILL

While these questions for evaluating cause-and-effect reasoning are being discussed, write them on the chalkboard. As with evaluating evidence, the students should be instructed to copy the questions into their notebooks and someone should make a poster to be put up in the classroom. For further discussion of this skill, refer students to the **Cause-and-Effect Reasoning** section of the "Guide to Critical Thinking" (pp. 5–7 in their text).

USING THE WORKSHEET

Once you have laid out the steps in evaluating cause-and-effect reasoning you can pass out Worksheet E for students to try for guided practice. When they have completed the worksheet, have them compare answers in small groups or in a whole-class discussion.

Suggested Answers

1.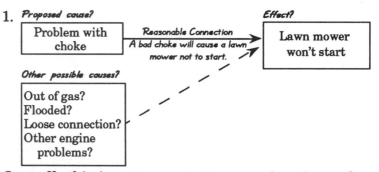

Overall, this is not very strong reasoning since other possible causes have not been ruled out.

2.

Overall, this is very strong reasoning since other possible causes have been ruled out.

3.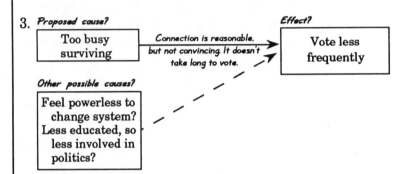

Overall, the other possible causes seem as important to the effect as the proposed cause. It is not a very strong argument.

Worksheet F: Comparison Arguments

Objectives

To introduce criteria for evaluating comparisons

Teaching Ideas

INTRODUCING THE SKILL

Have students do the introductory problem first. Make sure they write down their questions, then discuss the problem as a class.

After they have given their answers to the autocross problem, ask students what questions they ask to evaluate comparisons in general? (How are the two cases different?) If necessary, refer students to the section on **Comparisons** in the "Guide to Critical Thinking" (pp. 7–8 in the student text).

USING THE WORKSHEET

When students are ready to evaluate the comparison arguments, have them write their answers individually, then discuss the problems in small groups. Note to students that in Problem 3, since Candice is arguing that the radios are different, the students should focus on identifying similarities.

Suggested Answers

INTRODUCTORY PROBLEM

Some Autocross Race questions to ask:

1. What kind of car were you driving?

2. Was it the same course?

3. What were the weather conditions?

Emphasize to the students that they already know how to evaluate comparison arguments. They just showed it by the questions they asked.

COMPARISONS

1. Margarine substitute

— Compared: butter and margarine

— Possible differences: taste; amount or type of fat

— Possible similarities: function in baking

— Overall: They are similar enough to allow the cake to still come out as a cake, although there might be some difference in taste and texture. To demonstrate the similarities between butter and margarine, ask students what would happen if they substituted jelly for butter.

2. Statewide test

— Compared: student performance on one test at Centralville and Evantown

— Possible differences:

a. The student body of the two schools might be very different. For example, students might vary in educational background, ethnic background, economic opportunities, or social class.

b. The test may have been given in different grades in the two schools.

c. The curriculum at Centralville might be more suited to the test.

d. Testing circumstances at the two schools may have differed; e.g., physical testing environment; attitudes of students toward test; school activities before or after test, etc.

—Possible similarities: All above items might be similar rather than different.

—Overall: Not enough information is given. If most or all of the above items are different, then the comparison is very weak.

3. Deluxe Radio

—Compared: deluxe and standard radio models

—Possible differences: Cost is the only known difference; number of stations and sound quality are implied differences.

—Possible similarities: We don't know if the standard radio can also do the things the deluxe model can do.

—Overall: Candice has not drawn a reasonable conclusion. She may be satisfied with the radio, but she has not shown that the extra $50 was worth it. If the standard radio plays all the stations she likes and has a clear sound, then Candice's money was not well spent. In this comparison, the possible similarities undermine the argument because Candice is arguing they are different and that the difference makes the extra money spent worthwhile.

Worksheet G: Understanding Comparisons

Objectives

To identify comparison reasoning
To evaluate comparison arguments

Teaching Ideas

Have students write their answers individually, then discuss and defend their answers in small groups. Or you can discuss answers as a class.

Suggested Answers

• Numbers **1** and **5** are comparisons. Other items may have comparisons implied in them, but the comparison is not a key part of the argument.

8. A	11. D	14. D
9. D	12. A	
10. D	13. A	

15. a. Compares John's taste in movies to mine.

   b. It's an alike comparison.

   c. Since John is different from me in some ways, his taste in movies is likely to be different from mine in some ways.

   d. If John's movie taste is different from mine in a way that's important for this movie, then it might be a poor comparison. For example, if John doesn't mind violence in movies but I do, and if this movie is violent, then the comparison argument is faulty.

16. a. Compares Wranglers' team record to Panthers' team record.

   b. It's a different comparison (claims that since they are different from each other in a particular way, they are different in other particular ways also).

   c. Additional information would be needed in the areas of number of games and opponents. They may be similar or different.

   d. The more similarities that are found between the two teams, the stronger the argument that the Wranglers' team is better.

17. a. Compares state university to private college.

   b. It's an alike comparison.

c. Areas of possible comparison might include social life, facilities, library sources, cost, etc.

d. Maybe other aspects of the private college are better. On the other hand, if the campus and professors are the most important considerations to Carrie, then this is a good comparison.

18. a. Compares the private college to public colleges. (The comparison is implicit in "extra money.")

b. It is a difference comparison.

c–d. Since the statement doesn't say that the soccer team and the professors are better than at other, less expensive schools, there is no basis for making the claim that the extra money was worth it.

Worksheet H: Evaluating Generalizations

Objectives

To recognize and evaluate generalizations

Teaching Ideas
  USING THE WORKSHEET

The first worksheet section focuses on evaluating generalization claims. A circle diagram is shown for the example problem. If students find such diagrams helpful, encourage them to draw their own for problems 1–3.

The second section of the worksheet focuses on how far given information may be generalized. There is room for reasonable disagreement on these questions, so try to avoid pushing for one right answer. Ask students for the reasons for their answers. Focus on the subgroups of the major group in the generalization.

You might want to have the class read over the section on generalizations in the "Guide to Critical Thinking." If not, you can refer them to that section if they need help.

Suggested Answers

1. a. The generalization is that most kids in the school watch more than 12 hours of television a week.

    b. Subgroups might include honors, average, or remedial students; those involved in extracurricular activities and those who aren't; students who have jobs and those who don't; students from various income levels; students of various home environments; and so forth.

    c. The sample is relatively small (30 out of 800, or about 4%).

    d. The sample may have most of the subgroups by random distribution, but since it is a specific class, it is an ability group.

    e. This isn't a great sample because the amount of homework generally affects how much television a student watches. If this is a remedial class, the number of hours watched probably is not the same as the number of hours watched by honors students.

2. a. The generalization is that all Italians belong to the Mafia.

    b. Subgroups include different intelligence levels; different levels of education, income, and occupation; different geographic locations; different family lives and background; and so forth.

c. The sample may be exceedingly small (this person may know one Italian who belongs to the Mafia), somewhat larger (the person may live in an Italian neighborhood and know many Italians), or nonexistent (the person may have heard that Italians belong to the Mafia). Even with the larger sample, however, it is very small compared to the millions of Italians in the world.

d. We don't know much about the sample, but we can say with reasonable assurance that not all the subgroups are represented well.

e. This is a poor generalization. It is a good example of a stereotype—a large, complex group of people being simplified to all having a particular characteristic.

3. a. The generalization is that the population of Mudville rose dramatically in the 1970s.

b. As far as we know, the sample covers everyone in the large group (Mudville).

c. The generalization is very strong, which tells us that census records are good sources.

4. Neither A nor D are reasonable extensions of the information in your sample since both contain nonpublic, nonsuburban, and nonsecondary schools. (Is homework a key to good grades in elementary schools?) B, although restricted to your own suburban district, is weak for one of the same reasons that A and D are weak: it includes elementary schools. C is the best of the given choices. It is restricted to public suburban high schools, although it does extend the sample generalization too far geographically.

5. D is the best choice since it is the only one that emphasizes both the mountains and a strong defense. A emphasizes only defense, and it is unclear how being large or small affects avoiding war (B and C).

6. A is the best choice. The students in your school may be different (for example, in terms of educational or cultural background) from those in other schools, which makes it difficult to extend the sample beyond your own school (B and C). The information you have says nothing about the type of music students do not like.

Worksheet I: Identifying Unstated Assumptions — 1

Objectives

To recognize arguments based on assumptions
To identify assumptions made by others

Teaching Ideas

INTRODUCING THE SKILL

To encourage students to begin recognizing their own assumptions, give half the class statement 1 and the other half statement 2. Ask them to write an answer to the question. Don't say they have different statements.

1. "The Soviet Union gives a great deal of economic aid to India." Why do you think the Soviet Union does this?

2. "The United States gives a great deal of economic aid to India." Why do you think the United States does this?

When each student has written a response, list the various reasons on the chalkboard and ask the students to count the number of positive and negative motives attributed to each country. Were more positive motives given to the United States? If so, why?

Students may contend that the Soviet Union is an expansionist country which is trying to spread communism. The question "How do you know they are expansionist?" will force them to examine how they arrived at their belief. Similarly, "How do you know the United States is giving aid for humanitarian reasons?" will force them to question how they arrived at that belief. While it *may* be true that Soviet aid is self-serving and American aid is humanitarian, students should examine how they arrived at these beliefs. Did they have supporting evidence or did their frame of reference lead to the assumption?

USING THE WORKSHEET

It is probably better to start with this worksheet rather than Worksheet J. If students can identify the assumptions on this worksheet, then they probably do not need the more structured approach.

Suggested Answers

1. Your brother gets good grades in school because he studies. Your lower grades in school are due to lack of study (as opposed to other reasons).

2. Peter is the same age as (or older than) Marie.

3. You run faster than I do.

4. You don't have good writing skills.

5. I don't have other unexpected expenses. I'll be alive. I'll be able to drive.

6. Drinking is a way to enjoy life. Jim is too serious.

Worksheet J: Identifying Unstated Assumptions — 2

Objectives

To provide a structured approach to identifying assumptions in arguments

Teaching Ideas

It is probably a good idea to start assumptions with Introductory Worksheet I. If students can identify the assumptions in that worksheet, then they may not need this more structured approach. You may also choose to use this step-by-step approach with only a few students.

If you do use this worksheet, have the students discuss problem 1 as a class before they go on. Give students time to do problem 2 individually, then discuss their answers. Repeat this procedure for problem 3.

Suggested Answers

2. Step 1: (Premise) "Because" Fred works for a station which does fine work...

    Step 2: (Conclusion) "Therefore," Fred is a good mechanic.

    Step 3: (Unique parts) works for a station which does fine work/good mechanic

    Step 4: (Assumption) "People" who work for a station which does fine mechanical work must be good mechanics.

3. Step 1: (Premise) "Because" Sequoia is in the band (and Leona isn't)...

    Step 2: (Conclusion) "Therefore," Sequoia is a better musician (than Leona).

    Step 3: (Unique parts) in the band/better musician

    Step 4: (Assumption) "People" who are in a band are better musicians (than those who aren't).

WORKSHEET A The Bermuda Triangle

(1) The Bermuda Triangle—an area roughly from Bermuda, southwest to Florida, then east out into the Atlantic, and then northwest back to Bermuda—is one of the most dangerous and strange spots on earth. Beginning back in the 1600s and continuing to today, the number of ships lost in the Triangle is staggering. In recent years an average of about one hundred ships and many airplanes have been lost in the area each year. It is common knowledge among commercial pilots and ship captains that the Triangle is a dangerous place.

(2) What has happened to these boats and planes is especially mysterious, however, and that is what gives the area its name as the "Devil's Triangle." For example, a boat named the *Hollyhock* was off the coast of Florida when it suddenly lost radio contact with the coast. Later, it picked up California on the radio. Then it spotted land on its monitors where there was no land! The *Hollyhock* disappeared without a trace.

(3) Another boat, the *Witchcraft*, was at Buoy Number 7, only two miles off the coast of Miami, when the owner radioed to the Coast Guard for assistance because the boat was taking on water. He reassured the Coast Guard, however, that the boat was in no serious danger for it had built-in flotation chambers. When the Coast Guard arrived at Buoy Number 7, the *Witchcraft* had vanished.

(4) Airplanes, too, have had bizarre incidents. The *Star Tiger*, flying over the Devil's Triangle, suddenly lost all radio contact. No wreckage of the plane was ever found. In 1963 two KC-135 jet tankers disappeared three hundred miles southwest of Bermuda. What caused these planes to go down?

(5) Probably the most incredible incident concerned Training Flight 19, which took off from Fort Lauderdale, Florida, on December 5, 1945. Five Avenger aircraft took off that day on a regular Navy training flight. Pilot Cosner did not go on the flight. Why not? Commander Taylor also seemed hesitant. Did he have the same peculiar feeling as Cosner? The flight was routine at first, but then mysterious things started to happen. The pilots seemed confused and their instruments were doing weird things. The air base which had radio contact with the planes heard the pilots say, "Which way is west?" and the phrases "upside down" and "white water." The planes kept changing directions, almost flying in circles. Then—silence. A search plane was sent out and it, too, disappeared. The Navy has kept the incident quiet, and it hasn't denied the stories that authors have written about it.

(6) It is difficult to explain what happens in the Devil's Triangle. Some people believe there is a magnetic field which throws everything off. Others believe it has to do with the lost continent of Atlantis. Whatever the cause, it is worth thinking twice before traveling through this area—one of the strangest spots on our earth.

Relevant Information on the Bermuda Triangle

1. The *Star Tiger*'s flight was at night in poor weather.

2. It is not unheard of, although it is infrequent, for boats out in the ocean to pick up distant areas on the radio.

3. Rain clouds can sometimes look like land on radar.

4. The *Witchcraft* was out in bad weather.

5. Coast Guard reports make no mention of the *Witchcraft* being near Buoy Number 7. An author estimated the location by comparing several reports.

6. It would have taken the Coast Guard about twenty minutes to get from their station to where the *Witchcraft* was.

7. In twenty minutes a boat in calm seas can drift about one mile.

8. It is extremely difficult to find the wreckage of a plane or boat in the ocean, even on a clear day.

9. Debris found in one spot in the ocean contained the serial numbers of both KC-135 jet tankers. Some observers say this indicates that the two planes collided in the air.

10. The editor of *Aviation Week* stated that, based on a statistical analysis of the number of accidents in an area compared with the number of flights in that area, the Bermuda Triangle is one of the safest spots in the world. It is a popular area with pilots.

11. An Avenger aircraft will sink into the ocean roughly forty-five seconds after splashing down.

12. Two of the men who were in the radio tower in Fort Lauderdale at the time of Training Flight 19 do not recall the Avenger pilots saying "Which way is west?" or "upside down" or "white water." These two men say the planes were definitely lost.

13. Commander Taylor of Training Flight 19 radioed, "If we fly north, then east, we'll get home." He also mentioned being over the Keys (islands). He may have thought he was over the Florida Keys, when actually he was over the Grand Keys in the Atlantic. His proposed course of "north, then east" would have taken the planes toward the middle of the Atlantic.

14. At the time that radio contact was lost with the plane sent to search for Training Flight 19, people on the coast saw what looked like an explosion near the search plane's last-reported location.

15. Out of 10,000 distress calls made to the Coast Guard in that area, about 100 ships are lost in the Bermuda Triangle each year.

16. According to the Coast Guard, many pleasure boat owners don't know what they're doing in the ocean. For example, when the Coast Guard told one owner to plot a course toward an island, the owner said he couldn't find it on his map. The Coast Guard asked him what map he was using, and he said he was looking at the world atlas.

17. Each author who writes about the Bermuda Triangle describes a triangle of a different size and shape from the other authors.

18. The author of this Bermuda Triangle article writes books on popular subjects, such as mysterious and bizarre phenomena.

WORSHEET B   Evaluating Evidence

Background

You, as a historian, are trying to decide who stabbed John Jones in 1940 in the corridor at your school. You have gathered the following information (evidence) about the case.

Relevant Information

A.   The report on the police investigation into the death of John Jones says:
   1. The police concluded that he died of stab wounds.
   2. The police had three suspects: 1) Kid Kelly, 2) Slim Stowell, and 3) Lucky Levin. All three were in the corridor within ten feet of Jones when he was murdered.
   3. Police thought they had enough evidence to prosecute Lucky Levin.
B.   Lucky Levin was tried for the alleged murder of John Jones. In the trial:
   4. Lucky's girlfriend said he was a good person and would never kill anyone.
   5. A teacher testified he opened the door of his room and entered the corridor as soon as he heard John Jones scream. No one could have moved, and no one was moving when he looked into the corridor. Jones was lying on the floor while Lucky, Kid, and Slim were standing within ten feet, looking at him. Lucky was closest to Jones.
   6. Kid testified that he didn't do it, but he was looking the other way so he doesn't know whether Lucky or Slim did it.
   7. Slim testified that he didn't do it, Lucky did it.
   8. Lucky testified that he didn't do it, Slim did it.
   9. Witness A, who didn't know any of the men, said he heard Jones say, "No, Lucky, no" right before the murder.
   10. Witness B, who was 35 feet away and who didn't know any of the men, said he saw Lucky stab Jones.
   11. The knife was shown to have Lucky's, and only Lucky's, fingerprints on it.
   12. According to Kid, both Lucky and Slim had knives with them on the day of the death.
   13. The police found a knife on Slim at the scene of the murder, as well as the knife in Jones. No other weapons were found.
   14. An IOU note produced at the trial showed that Jones owed Lucky $300, which had been due to be paid three days before the murder.
   15. Witness C testified that Slim did not like Jones.
   16. Witness D, 50 feet away, testified that she saw Lucky stab Jones.
   17. Witness E, in another part of the building and not within sight of the murder scene, says he's sure Lucky killed Jones.
   18. At the trial, a letter from Lucky's girlfriend to her mother was introduced as evidence. The letter said that Lucky hated John Jones.
C.   The jury found Lucky guilty of murder.

Evaluate the Evidence

Q As a historian, do you think the jury was right in its verdict? Why do you think so?

Q Give one example from the Relevant Information section on page 33 for each type of evidence listed below. Write the number of the evidence on the line provided.

_____A. Statements by witnesses

_____B. Documents (written information)

_____C. Objects

Q Evaluate (judge) the following evidence selected from the Relevant Information. Use the **PROP** factors (criteria) from the section on **Evidence** in the "Guide to Critical Thinking" (pp. 2–4).

Factor #	4	7	10	11	14	17	18
P							
R							
O							
P							

Q Compare the reliability of evidence 4 and evidence 18. Which is more reliable? Explain your answer.

WORKSHEET C   Sources and Evidence

Whenever you see information used in support of an argument you should ask certain questions, the first and most important being, "Does the information have a source given?"

A *source* is the person, place, or written document the information came from. If there is no given source, the information cannot be evaluated and should not be accepted as reliable.

If the information does give a source, you can evaluate its reliability by asking a number of questions, four of which are given here. For further help, see the section on **Evidence** in the "Guide to Critical Thinking."

Criteria for Evaluating Evidence

P   Is it a **primary** (more reliable) or secondary (less reliable) source?

R   Does the person giving the evidence have any **reason to lie** (less reliable)?

O   Is there **other evidence** which supports or verifies what this evidence says (more reliable) or is this the only evidence presented on the topic (less reliable)?

P   Is it a public (less reliable) or **private** (more reliable) statement? It is public if the person giving it knew other people would read or see it.

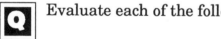 Evaluate each of the following arguments using the above questions.

1.   The city government under Mayor Elwell was very corrupt. Over $15 million was stolen in only five years.

   Is there a source given for any information in this argument? _____
   If not, the claim of corruption is not well supported by evidence.
   If yes, evaluate the evidence and explain your evaluation.

   P

   R

   O

   P

2. Kurt is a great hitter. The statistics from last season's scorebook show he hit .457, a very high average.

    Is there a source given for any information in this argument? _____

    If not, the argument is not well supported. If yes, evaluate it.

    P

    R

    O

    P

3. The city government under Mayor Pratt was very corrupt. Three city workers stated in public hearings that they each had seen money paid to city officials for special favors.

    Is there a source given for any information in this argument? _____

    If not, the argument is not well supported. If yes, evaluate it.

    P

    R

    O

    P

4. Kelley is a great hitter. She can hit the fast ball and the curve.

    Is there a source given for any information in this argument? _____

    If not, the argument is not well supported. If yes, evaluate it.

    P

    R

    O

    P

WORKSHEET D   Evaluating Evidence — PROP

You will recall that the first question you should ask about information (evidence) is whether or not a source is given. Each argument on this worksheet names the source, or the person who said it. For further explanation see the section on **Evidence** in the "Guide to Critical Thinking."

Criteria for Evaluating Evidence

P   Is it a **primary** (more reliable) or secondary (less reliable) source?

R   Does the person giving the evidence have any **reason to lie** (less reliable)?

O   Is there **other evidence** which supports or verifies what this evidence says (more reliable) or is this the only evidence presented on the topic (less reliable)?

P   Is it a public (less reliable) or **private** (more reliable) statement? It is public if the person giving it knew other people would read or see it.

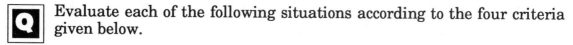 Evaluate each of the following situations according to the four criteria given below.

1.   Yu-chi tells his father it was not his fault that he got detention. He said that the teacher thought he was talking during class, but he wasn't.

Evaluate Yu-chi's evidence according to the four criteria.

P

R

O

P

Overall, how reliable is Yu-chi's evidence?

2. Bob is angry because he thinks his girlfriend, Jill, went out with Larry on Friday. Laura, Connie, and Ellen all told Bob that they had talked with Jill on the phone most of the night on Friday while she was baby-sitting, so she couldn't have gone out with Larry.

Evaluate Laura's evidence according to the four criteria.

P

R

O

P

Overall, how reliable is Laura's evidence?

3. Christie tells her parents she failed English because she didn't study. She says she has no one to blame but herself and has to admit she deserves to be grounded.

Evaluate Christie's evidence about why she failed.

P

R

O

P

Overall, how reliable is Christie's evidence?

 ©1993 CRITICAL THINKING PRESS & SOFTWARE, P.O. BOX 448, PACIFIC GROVE, CA 93950

WORKSHEET E   Cause-and-Effect Reasoning

When someone proposes a cause for some situation or event, he or she is using cause-and-effect reasoning. Following these steps will help you evaluate such arguments.

EVALUATING CAUSE-AND-EFFECT REASONING

1. Decide which is the cause and which is the effect.

2. See if the person explains how the cause led to the effect. If the person doesn't explain, we should ask if there is a reasonable connection between the cause and the effect.

3. Ask if there are other possible causes for this effect. Has this person eliminated these other possible causes?

Q Using a diagram like the one shown after the first problem will help you follow these steps when evaluating cause-and-effect reasoning. Draw your own diagrams for the other problems.

1. The repairman says that Mark's lawn mower won't start because of a problem with the choke, which will cost $25.00 to fix.

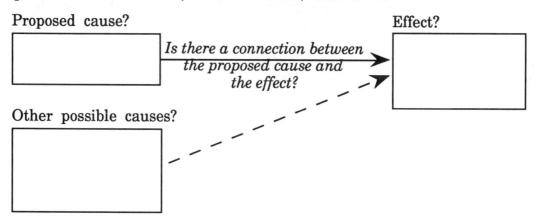

Overall, how strong is the repairman's cause-and-effect reasoning?

---

2. Mr. Alberti insulated his house before this winter started. The average temperature this winter has been about the same as last winter, and Mr. Alberti has kept the thermostat at the same settings both winters. So far, he has used 40% fewer gallons of oil than he had at this time last winter. He thinks the insulation has been very effective in saving heating oil.

    Analyze Mr. Alberti's cause-and-effect thinking. Use a diagram.

    Overall, how strong is the argument?

3. Low-income people tend to vote less frequently than high-income people because poorer people are so busy trying to survive that they don't take time to vote.

    Draw a diagram and analyze this thinking.

    Overall, how strong is the argument?

WORKSHEET F   Comparison Arguments

Introductory Problem

> Suppose you drove in an autocross race at the North Shore Shopping Center parking lot a month ago. ("Autocross" is a race over a winding course set up with cone markers. Cars race one at a time and are clocked as they run the course.) You drove your 1952 Plymouth, and your time was 36.8 seconds. Now, suppose Harry told you that last Sunday he was in an autocross and his time was 28.2 seconds. He says this proves he is a better driver than you are.

Write three questions that you would want to ask Harry.

1.

2.

3.

Evaluating Comparison Arguments

A comparison argument reasons that since two cases are similar in some respects they will also be similar in another way. You can tell from the questions you wrote above that the key to deciding the strength of a comparison argument is asking, "How are the two cases different?" Refer to the section on **Comparison Reasoning** in the "Guide to Critical Thinking" (Unit 1) if you need more help.

 Using the given questions, evaluate each of the following comparison arguments.

1. You are baking a cake and the recipe calls for 5 teaspoons of butter. You have no butter, so you reason that if you substitute 5 teaspoons of margarine the cake will still turn out fine.

   a.   What two items are being compared?

   b.   How are they different?

   c.   How are they alike?

   d.   Overall, how strong is this comparison argument?

---

2. The average score on the statewide test was 12 points higher at Centralville High than it was at Evantown High. It is clear from these scores that the teachers at Centralville are doing a better job of teaching.

    a. What two items are being compared?

    b. How are they different?

    c. How are they alike?

    d. Overall, how strong is this comparison argument?

3. Candice paid $50 more to get the deluxe model when she bought her radio. She thinks the money was well spent because the radio gets all the stations she likes and the sound is very clear.

    a. What two items are being compared?

    b. How are they different?

    c. How are they alike?

    d. Overall, how strong is this comparison argument?

WORKSHEET G   Understanding Comparisons

For help, refer to the section about **Comparisons** in the "Guide to Critical Thinking."

Identifying Comparisons

Q Put a "C" on the line in front of each of the following arguments or claims that use comparison reasoning.

_____ 1.   Jean felt that the suede jacket was worth the extra money.

_____ 2.   Benji has been a great dog. He's very obedient and he doesn't bark much.

_____ 3.   Fred used his new equipment the last time he climbed.

_____ 4.   I decided to read *A Tale of Two Cities* because, although it is long, it is an excellent story.

_____ 5.   You should buy alkaline batteries; they last longer than regular ones.

_____ 6.   Tom and Pat helped us out a lot when we had to fix the house. They are good neighbors.

_____ 7.   Tomika hit the other car when she backed up in the parking lot.

Categorizing Comparisons

Q Mark each of the following arguments. Put an **S** in front of arguments which claim that the two cases are basically similar. Put a **D** in front of arguments which claim that the two cases are basically different. Remember, better/worse comparisons emphasize differences.

_____ 8.   You gave Mari $5.00 for her work, so you should give me $5.00 for my work, too.

_____ 9.   Since our team has won more games this year than last, we must have improved.

_____ 10.   Rachel is the right player to guard their scorer. Julie just isn't as good on defense.

_____ 11.   The new deluxe sedan costs a little more but it's well worth it. It has cruise control and an engine.

_____ 12.   I beat George at chess last time, so I'm sure I will again.

_____ 13.   Jim has never charged us more than $50.00 for a repair in the past, so he surely won't charge us too much this time.

_____ 14.   I'm sticking with Toni because she's a better computer programmer than Geoffrey is.

Analyzing and Evaluating Comparisons

 Each of the following problems presents a comparison argument for you to analyze and evaluate. The **Example** is done for you.

Example:

"I jumped 5'6" in the last meet, so I should jump at least 5'6" today.

    a.   What are the two cases or characteristics being compared?

        Case A: [the speaker's jumping ability at the last meet]

        Case B: [the speaker's jumping ability today]

    b.   Is this an alike or different comparison?

        [Alike]

    c.   What similarities or differences are there between the two cases?

        [Similarities: same goal in same event]

        [Differences: the jumper's health or condition may be different today; weather, jumping conditions, or training time may differ]

    d.   How strong is the comparison?

        [It's reasonable, but it should take into account the possible differences. For example, if the jumper claimed to be in better condition now and the weather is favorable, then the conclusion would be stronger.]

15.   "My best friend, John, liked the movie, so I bet I'll like it too."

    a.   What are the two cases or characteristics being compared? Be precise!

        Case A:

        Case B:

    b.   Is this an alike or different comparison?

    c.   What similarities or differences are there between the two cases?

    d.   How strong is the comparison?

16.   "The Wranglers have a better team than the Panthers. The Wranglers have more wins and fewer losses."

    a.   What are the two cases or characteristics being compared?

        Case A:

        Case B:

    b.   Is this an alike or different comparison?

c.   What similarities or differences are there between the two cases?

d.   How strong is the comparison?

17.   Carrie decided that the state university is just as good as the private college in her area. The campus and the professors at the state university are as good as those at the private college.

a.   What are the two cases or characteristics being compared?

Case A:

Case B:

b.   Is this an alike or different comparison?

c.   What similarities or differences are there between the two cases?

d.   How strong is the comparison?

18.   Roger decides that the extra money he spends to attend the private college is well worth it. The soccer team is excellent at the private college, as are the professors.

a.   What are the two cases or characteristics being compared?

Case A:

Case B:

b.   Is this an alike or different comparison?

c.   What similarities or differences are there between the two cases?

d.   How strong is the comparison?

WORKSHEET H   Evaluating Generalizations

If you need help, refer to the definition and examples of **Generalization** in the "Guide to Critical Thinking." Remember that a circle diagram is useful to help visualize generalizations as an analysis aid. An example is done for you.

Example:

"Most American adults would like to own their own homes. Just last month a survey of 1232 students at five hundred colleges around the country showed that 62% of those students who responded want to own their own home."

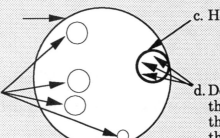

a. What generalization is being made about the whole group?

b. What subgroups make up the whole group?

c. How large is the sample?

d. Does the sample have all the same subgroups in the same proportion as the whole group?

a. Generalization?
[Most American adults want to own homes.]

b. Subgroups of whole group?
[Subgroups include men and women and various geographic regions, ages, incomes, and levels of education.]

c. Size of sample?
[The sample is rather small, compared to the number of people in the whole group, so representativeness will be important.]

d. Representativeness of sample?
[The sample includes men and women (probably) from different geographic regions, but is not representative in any other way. The sample consists of people who are young, have a relatively high level of income, and have a uniformly high level of education.]

e. Overall, how strong is the generalization?
[This is a very weak sample; therefore, it is not a good generalization.]

Q Evaluate the following generalizations. Draw a circle graph and use the given questions to help with your evaluation.

1. "Most students in this high school [800 students] watch more than twelve hours of television a week. We took a poll in my social studies class, and twenty out of the thirty students said they watch more than twelve hours a week." [This school has honors, average, and remedial classes.]

    a. Generalization?

    b. Subgroups of whole group?

    c. Size of sample?

    d. Representativeness of sample?

    e. Strength of generalization?

2. "I wouldn't hire an Italian if I were you. They all belong to the **Mafia**. Pretty soon you'll start having problems."
    a. Generalization?

    b. Subgroups of whole group?

    c. Size of sample?

    d. Representativeness of sample?

    e. Strength of generalization?

3. "The 1980 census [a survey of every household in the country] showed that the population of Mudville rose dramatically during the 1970s."
    a. Generalization?

    b. Subgroups of whole group?

    c. Size of sample?

    d. Representativeness of sample?

    e. Strength of generalization?

Write the letter of the most reasonable generalization on the line in front of each item. Explain your choice in the space provided.

_____4.   Suppose you found that in your public, suburban high school, those students who do more homework also get better grades. Which of the following is the best generalization to make from this information?

    A.   In your state, students who do more homework get better grades.

    B.   In your school district, students who do more homework get better grades.

    C.   In public, suburban high schools in the United States, students who do more homework get better grades.

    D.   Students who do more homework get better grades.

Explain your choice.

_____5.   Suppose you knew that Switzerland, which is a small, mountainous country, has used a strong defense (large military) to successfully avoid war. Which of the following is the best generalization to make from this information?

    A.   A large military is the key to avoiding war.

    B.   Small countries can use a strong defense to avoid war.

    C.   Large countries can use a strong defense to avoid war.

    D.   Mountainous countries can avoid war through building a strong defense.

Explain your choice.

_____6.   You know that 75% of the kids in your ninth-grade homeroom like rock music best. Which of the following is the best generalization to make from this information?

    A.   Most ninth-graders in your school like rock music best.

    B.   Anywhere you go in the country, you'll find that most teenagers like rock music best.

    C.   All ninth-grade students like rock music best.

    D.   Few ninth-grade students in your school like classical music.

Explain your choice.

 ©1993 Critical Thinking Press & Software, P.O. Box 448, Pacific Grove, CA 93950

WORKSHEET I   Identifying Unstated Assumptions — 1

What are the unstated assumptions in each of the following arguments? If you need help, look at the section on **Assumptions** in the "Guide to Critical Thinking."

1.   "Why can't you study like your brother? He gets all A's in school."

2.   "Beth is older than Peter, so she must be older than Marie also."

3.   "Even if I have a head start running to the beach, you'll get there first."

4.   "Are you sure you want to apply for that job? It requires someone with good writing skills."

5.   "When I get my raise, I'm going to buy a new car."

6.   "Jim, why don't you come drinking with us? You've got to learn to relax and enjoy life."

WORKSHEET J   Identifying Unstated Assumptions — 2

This four-step approach is one method for identifying unstated assumptions.

Step 1	Write out the premise. (The premise is the part of an argument that tells "why" something is true. Look for the place to put "because." What follows is the premise.)
Step 2	Find and write out the conclusion of the argument. (Look for the place to put "therefore." What follows it is the conclusion.)
Step 3	Find the unique part of the conclusion (the part that doesn't appear in the premise) and the unique part of the premise (the part that doesn't appear in the conclusion.)
Step 4	Combine the two unique parts in a sentence that starts with a general word, such as people, wars, or countries. This sentence is the unstated assumption.

Q Try the four-step approach on the following claims. If you need help, look at the section on **Assumptions** in the "Guide to Critical Thinking." The first one is done for you as an example.

1. "Roger is not a football player since he weighs only 130 pounds."

    Step 1:   "Because" he weighs only 130 pounds. (Premise)

    Step 2:   "Therefore" Roger is not a football player. (Conclusion)

    Step 3:   …weighs only 130 pounds (P)/…not a football player (C)

    Step 4:   "People" who weigh only 130 pounds are not football players.

2. Fred is definitely a good mechanic. He works for the service station on Main Street which is known for its fine mechanical work.

    Step 1:

    Step 2:

    Step 3:

    Step 4:

3. Sequoia is in the band and Leona isn't, so Sequoia must be a better musician.

    Step 1:

    Step 2:

    Step 3:

    Step 4:

WORKSHEET K   Analyzing Historical Films

When watching a film or video interpretation of any event, consider using the following (**PIPER**) model of analysis.

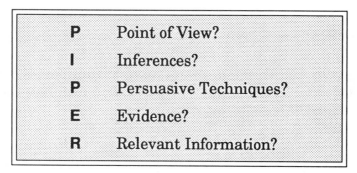

P	Point of View?
I	Inferences?
P	Persuasive Techniques?
E	Evidence?
R	Relevant Information?

Use this worksheet to help you analyze historical films you watch.

1. Name of film:

2. Main point of the film:

3. **P**   What is the **point of view** of the film? Was it overly favorable or critical of a particular group or individual?

4. **I**   What **inferences** were made in the film? Were there parts of the film that the filmmakers must have made up because they couldn't have known this from the available evidence?

5. **P**   What techniques are used in the film to **persuade** the audience to the filmmaker's point of view? Note camera angle, music, character portrayal, etc.

6. **E**   What **evidence** is included to support the point of view put forth in the film? What is the source of that evidence? How strong is it?

7. **R**   What **relevant information** do I know? Does it contradict or support the story presented in the film?

8. Overall, how strong are the historical arguments in this film? Is it historically accurate?

WORKSHEET L   Analyzing Historical Interpretations
Lesson _____   Interpretation _____

 Answer the following questions on each interpretation.

1.   What is the main idea of this interpretation?

2.   List two or three key points the author(s) use(s) to support the main idea, write any evidence given to support the point, and evaluate the evidence according to the **PROP** questions.

Key Point	Evidence that supports the point	Evaluation of Evidence
1		
2		

3.   Identify and analyze one cause-and-effect argument the interpretation makes. Fill in the cause and the effect first, then complete the diagram.

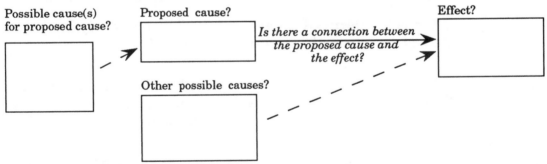

Overall, how strong is this cause-and-effect reasoning?

4.   Analyze any other aspect of the argument presented in the interpretation. For example, evaluate a generalization, comparison, or proof argument; identify an unstated assumption; note vague or emotional words that need to be defined more clearly by the author.

5.   If **Relevant Information** is provided, does any of the given information affect this interpretation? If so, identify the specific information by number(s) and state the effect(s) of each on the interpretation.

6.   What is your overall judgment of the interpretation? Identify its strengths and weaknesses.

UNIT 2
NEW REPUBLIC

Lesson 1: Identifying Sources

Objectives

To identify sources of information

Teaching Ideas

This is a simple lesson to give students practice in identifying sources of information. It can be assigned for homework and gone over in class, or it can be done entirely in class. In either case, it need not take a lot of class time. Students can break into small groups to compare their answers and then the whole class can discuss them fairly quickly.

Suggested Answers

1. S   *Time* is the source.

2. N

3. N

4. N

5. S   The source is *The Nation Takes Shape*.

6. N

7. S   Lewis and Clark's diaries are the sources.

8. S   *The Americans* is the source. This problem was included to introduce the idea of footnotes (or endnotes) for citing sources.

Lesson 2: Evaluating Sources

Objectives

To evaluate evidence according to specific criteria

Teaching Ideas

This is an introductory lesson on evaluating evidence according to three criteria: primary/secondary source, reason to lie, and corroboration. It is a basic lesson which breaks the task down and has students examine one criterion at a time. The lesson may be too step-by-step for more advanced students.

You can assign the lesson for homework, have students discuss their answers in small groups, and then discuss the answers as a class.

Suggested Answers

PRIMARY OR SECONDARY?

1. P   She saw it.

2. S

3. P   He explored the areas he described.

4. S/P? Currier and Ives may have seen that train, but the painting may be of their impressions of trains in general. On the other hand, the painting was from that time, so it would be considered a primary source by many people. If the question is, How did people view trains at that time? then the painting is definitely primary.

5. S   It's probably secondary, but it could be primary if the paper had its own reporter on the scene of the gold rush.

REASON TO LIE?

6. R   So she wouldn't be penalized.

7. R   To justify the request for war

8. N

9. R   Grundy may have thought his state would be helped by war.

10. N

CORROBORATION?

11. (#3) Pike's description could be checked by reading travel accounts, government reports, history books, or geographical surveys of the area.

12. (#7) Among others, you could check history books (secondary sources), naval records, newspapers, U.S. government records, or British records (primary sources) to corroborate President Madison's charges.

Lesson 3: Determining Causes and Effects

Objective

To identify cause and effect
To distinguish between causes and effects

Teaching Ideas

Have students read, if necessary, the introductory section on causal reasoning in the "Guide to Critical Thinking," Unit 1. Also, use the introductory exercise (Worksheet E) for this skill if you have not already done so.

Go over questions 1 and 2 to make sure students understand how to do the first section. Have students complete the rest of the first section (questions 3–8), discuss their answers in small groups, and discuss as a class.

Then repeat the same format for the second section (questions 9–12).

Suggested Answers

1. [C]

2. [E]

3. E

4. C   *Because* indicates cause.

5. C

6. E   *So* indicates effect.

7. E

8. C   *Due to* indicates cause.

9. N   No cause for why the restaurant is the busiest is proposed.

10. C   Cause: drought in the Midwest; effect: supply of wheat is smaller

11. C   Cause: depleted furs in the East; effect: trappers pushed inland

12. N   No cause for or effect of the expedition is proposed.

Lesson 4: Evaluating Cause-and-Effect Reasoning

Objectives

To evaluate cause and effect

Teaching Ideas

Have students individually answer question 1, then discuss their answers as a class. Have students, in small groups, do questions 2–8, then discuss as a class.

Suggested Answers

1. R   Some students may not see how TV violence causes people to be more violent, and this argument doesn't explain how. However, there are many studies which present evidence showing that it does cause people to be more violent.

2. R   It makes sense that accidents would be more severe, but it isn't explained here.

3. S   Here the arguer explains why a field-rotation system leads to a higher yield per acre.

4. Students should note a number of possible reasons why Alyssa might break up with John other than his not taking her to the prom.

5. There are other possible causes, such as Mexican actions or economic motives, but this argument does present several causes.

6. This argument explains the connection between winning the pennant (cause) and higher ticket prices (effect), and the argument makes a lot of sense (good connection). However, other economic factors, such as higher costs, higher incomes, or inflation, may also have caused the increase in ticket prices.

7. There is a very good connection, which is explained, between wiping out the buffalo (cause) and destroying the Plains Indians' way of life (effect). Other factors, such as environmental changes or warfare, may also have destroyed their way of life, but wiping out the buffalo is quite likely to be a very important cause.

8. Again the connection between the change in fashion (cause) and demise of the mountain man (effect) is explained reasonably well. However, another possible cause, wiping out of beaver, may have been just as important as the change in fashion.

Lesson 5: Identifying and Evaluating Comparisons

Objectives

To identify and evaluate comparisons

Teaching Ideas

The section on identifying comparisons should not be too difficult and can be done quickly. Cue students to watch for comparative words, as mentioned in the directions. The section on evaluating comparisons should be more challenging and may lead to some problematic responses. Try to focus on the process of evaluating comparisons rather than on right answers.

Suggested Answers

IDENTIFYING COMPARISONS

1. N

2. N

3. C   "Before" (sooner) sometimes indicates a comparison. It is a comparison in this example.

4. N

5. C   "Healthier" indicates a comparison.

6. N

7. N

EVALUATING COMPARISONS

8. There could be differences other than fertilization between the two sets of roses which could account for their larger size. For example, the roses could be of different varieties, or the soil could be different in the two pots. These other factors should be accounted for in the explanation to strengthen the comparison.

9. There is a very important difference which was argued in the actual case. Article 6 of the constitution calls federal law "the supreme law of the land." According to this line of reasoning, the federal government <u>can</u> do things which states cannot.

10. Some economists believe it is not in a country's economic interest to have tariffs even when other countries have tariffs. Tariffs always lead to inefficiency, and exchange rates will correct trade deficits, they argue. Other economists believe tariffs are necessary for protecting fragile industries. The arguments are complex and difficult, but they do show this comparison argument is questionable.

Lesson 6: How Did Early Industrialization Change Small New England Villages?

Objectives

To evaluate cause and effect
To evaluate evidence
To identify and evaluate generalizations

Teaching Ideas

As mentioned in the introduction in the student book, this lesson focuses on the changes brought to New England villages resulting from early industrialization.

Begin by asking students to list characteristics of their own community today. Discuss their answers and list them on the chalkboard, labeling them as economic, social, or political characteristics. Tell the class that historians look at groups or events from these various perspectives—economic, social, and political. In this lesson, students will have the opportunity to practice thinking like a historian by analyzing a town according to its social and economic characteristics.

Students should be familiar with basic economic and sociological concepts before starting their analysis. The handout (p. 39) provides a glossary of some of these concepts. Review them at the outset with the class, or have students refer to them as needed during the lesson.

Have students read the "Description of a New England Town, 1810" and fill in the questions under Part I—Before Industrialization. Then put students into small groups to compile group responses to the questions in Part I. After 5 or 10 minutes, have each group report to the class.

After you have discussed the economic and social characteristics of the town in 1810, have students fill in Part II of the lesson. Again, they can discuss their answers in small groups and then as a class.

Students now should read the diary excerpt in Part III and write down which items from Part I it confirms and which it weakens. They can continue by reading the Accounts of the Davis Family in Part IV and writing which items from Part II it confirms and which it weakens.

These industrial changes can be summarized by students in a short essay.

Students who are capable of analyzing without the structured questions should be asked simply to list four economic and four social characteristics, and then four economic and four social changes, resulting from the new factories.

Suggested Answers

PART I—BEFORE INDUSTRIALIZATION
A. ECONOMIC

1. Trade was done by barter and credit, little money was used.

2. Workers were not specialized.

3. Methods and tools were old and not very productive.

4. Workers had a range of skills.

5. Farming dominated.

B. SOCIAL

6. Cooperation was very important compared to individual initiative.

7. The family was very important—for example, work was organized around families.

8. The town was not very stratified—distance between the richest and the poorest was not as great as in the United States today. Mobility was limited but not as much as in societies where birth determined social class.

9. The work environment was the home and fields; nature and the workers set the schedule and pace.

10. Luxury items don't appear to have been very important. There is no mention of fancy clothes, homes or furnishings other than wallpaper.

PART II—CHANGES FROM SMALL FACTORIES
A. ECONOMIC

11. Money is now much more important since people have cash. Banking will become important not only due to the cash, but also because the new mills need loans.

12. Workers in the mills will be more specialized, mainly knowing how to run a few machines.

13. Knowledge as well as machines will be filtering into the town, so new methods of producing many things, including crops, will be sought. People will be trying to produce efficiently to maximize profits.

14. Workers who are running machines will be learning few skills. The number of less skilled workers will rise.

15. Farming will still be dominant but will gradually diminish in importance.

B. SOCIAL

16. The individual will become more important as machinery and specialization emerge. Hiring the specialist and his or her equipment is more likely to emphasize the individual, whereas the house raising emphasized the whole community.

17. The family will be less important as various family members earn cash outside the home. Parental control over their children, for example in marriage choices, will wane. The location of work itself outside the home shows the reduction of family control. In addition, employer and employee will now most likely not be related and possibly not know each other.

18. It might be less stratified in that anyone who wants to advance up the social ladder now has an opportunity, i.e., through investment. On the other hand, the distance between the top class (the owners) and the lowest class will be much greater, and owner and worker no longer know each other. Distinct capitalist (owner) and working classes might arise.

19. The work environment has shifted from natural surroundings to indoors in a factory. In addition, the work schedule and pace are set by the owner and bells, not by the worker and nature.

20. Since people have more cash, and the wealthiest people will be much wealthier than before, it is reasonable to speculate that luxury items will become much more important. Students might be interested in discussing the possibility that industrialization is an important cause of our consumer culture today.

PART III—SARAH ANNA
EMERY DIARY

21. The Emery diary confirms all of the hypotheses in Part I about village life, except stratification (#8) which can't be inferred from this diary. The aunt shares the milk, and there is no mention of money, which implies a barter arrangement. The workers do a number of chores related to farming, use simple methods, have a range of skills, and are organized around cooperative family work. The environment is home and field, and there is no mention of luxuries—few of the houses are painted.

22. Evaluation—This is a primary source. Since it is a diary (private so far as we know) there seems to be no reason to lie. On the other hand, it is written 50–60 years after the events occurred, which makes it less reliable. Other accounts with similar descriptions of

daily life would strengthen the reliability of this source. We also have to be careful not to generalize too far from this one diary. The description here might be accurate for the Emery family and even for other farm families in Newburyport. But families in different towns, or in different social classes, might be very different.

PART IV—ACCOUNTS OF THE DAVIS FAMILY

23. The Davis family accounts supports the following changes in village life:

- Workers will become less skilled and more specialized: when Mr. Davis is working at the mill, he is working with a machine which involves few skills. Meanwhile, he is not using farm skills as much.

- Farming is of less importance than before.

- The family is less important as some, but not all, of the family are working at the mill. Thus, family members are separated more often and are less dependent on each other for completing farm tasks.

- The work environment has changed to indoor factory work.

- The Davis's may have bought some luxury items at the company store, but it can't be inferred here.

Interestingly, the store was run on credit, as stores had been traditionally run before industrialization. There is no mention of cash, so maybe all wages were paid in credit.

24. The accounts record of the Davis family is a primary source, and it is difficult to see why anything would have been altered or withheld, so there doesn't seem to be a reason to lie. There is no corroborating evidence for the Davis accounts.

Lesson 7: What Were the Characteristics of the Ideal Woman in the Early 1800s?

Objectives

To evaluate visual evidence
To identify and evaluate generalizations

Teaching Ideas

This lesson is about women's roles and perceptions of women in the early to mid-19th century (1810–1860).

Have students look over the two pictures in Part I and then do activities 1–4.

For activity 1, have students get into groups of three (try to mix males and females in each group), and have each group compile one list of characteristics of women in the early 1800s. Allow 4 or 5 minutes for this activity. Then ask: What was the expected role of women as shown in the pictures?

After 4 or 5 minutes on question 1, have each group star the characteristics which are still true for women today. Discuss both lists as a class. Be alert to prevent the discussion from degenerating into a girls versus boys debate.

Now move on to activity 3 and discuss as a class how accurate these pictures (which were taken from *The Ladies Cabinet of Fashion* and another magazine) are in showing women's actual roles and society's perceptions of women's roles. (This question asks students to evaluate the pictures as sources and evaluate their representativeness for generalizing about women in the early to mid-1800s.)

Ask students: What would pictures of men and children in the early 1800s (1810–1860) have looked like? What were expected roles of men and children?

Assign activity 4 for homework. Ask students to find at least one picture from their text, or any other source, of a man or child from the early 1800s and list the characteristics shown in the picture. Or ask them to find pictures of women showing them in different roles. They should bring the picture or a copy of the picture to class.

In the next class, have students share their pictures and lists of characteristics. There should be some differences in the pictures (some fashionably dressed, others dressed as mountain men, etc.) which should help students recognize some of the pitfalls of generalizing from only a few sources. Discuss the roles of women and men and the tentative nature of the students' lists.

Ask students: How could we check further to substantiate our hypotheses about the expected role of women in American society in the early 1800s? (We could check newspapers, magazines, and books from that era, for example; or we could check men's and women's letters and diaries.)

Have students read Part II and answer the questions that follow. These quotes were culled from the magazines and books listed. The quotes will, no doubt, substantiate some student hypotheses about the role of women, and will introduce some new characteristics. Discuss student responses to the questions.

One way to conclude the lesson is to have students find pictures of men, women, and children today and have them explain expected roles based on the pictures. A second evaluation is to have students write a short essay: "Male/Female Roles—Then and Now."

Suggested Answers

1. Many characteristics could be listed. Students should note the role of women as objects—as something to look at, noting especially the restrictive nature of the corset and other clothing. The corset was apparently comfortable to some women and extremely debilitating to others. The corset forced internal organs to move in some women, causing damage and great pain when it was removed. There are several cases where women's deaths are attributed to the effects of corsets. Whether comfortable or medically harmful, it is important to note that women wore them generally without complaint. Women seemed to accept their role and in many cases actively promoted it.

2. Some students will see that women are still viewed as objects—something to look good. They will argue that little has really changed, women are still subservient, docile, fragile, and manipulated. Other students will point out the many changes in women's role in society: in work, leisure, dress, insurance laws, property ownership, and so forth. Cut off digressions into debates or diatribes on present-day issues, such as abortion. The issues can be raised but not discussed in depth since no study is being done on present-day issues in this lesson.

3. Most students will subconsciously draw conclusions about women in general from the two pictures. This is dangerous for a number of reasons. First, the pictures show women in regard only to fashionable dress. Pictures of women working on farms or in homes would look very different and depict different roles, for example. Second, these pictures may only apply to a particular class (middle or upper class) or a particular region (Northeast). Third, they apply only to white women. Did students generalize that *women* in America in the early 1800s had such and such characteristics? How well do these characteristics apply to black women (mostly slaves), Hispanics, Native Americans, or even newly arrived immigrants?

The pictures themselves are primary sources. The magazines, of course, have reason to exaggerate women's role in particular ways in order to sell corsets or other products. And because magazines portrayed women a certain way does not mean women saw themselves that way. On the other hand, the magazine pictures do represent some people's perceptions of women's roles. And if the portrayal in the magazines were very different from their readers' perceptions the magazine might lose readers, so the magazine probably represents the views or perceptions of many of its readers.

4. What students list will depend on what they find. Are men viewed in textbooks as more active and decisive than women? Are they shown in leadership roles? This is a good point to discuss the political nature of textbooks. Women's groups have been critical of history texts for their portrayal of women, so textbook publishers made some changes (often still unsatisfactory to women's groups). Other minority groups have likewise been critical, stimulating other changes. The important point about history texts (as well as any other history works) is that the information in them is selected. People disagree about what should be included, and they argue about who should do the selecting.

5–6. In answering question 5 and 6, students can add characteristics to their lists from their answers to question 1 and 2. You might want to ask what roles are designated for men as well. The discussion of roles should be lively.

7. These documents have the same strengths and weaknesses as the pictures, as described in the answer to question 3. One difference is there are more documents here from a variety of magazines and books. To what extent do these represent what women read then? What was the literacy rate among American women? (Very high.) How extensive was the readership of these sources? Were there other magazines portraying a different set of characteristics for women? Students should always be asking themselves, "What's left out, what's not included here that might paint a different picture?" These documents could have been selected to give a particular impression of women in the early 1800s, while leaving out other documents giving a different impression—the fallacy of special pleading (student book, p. 11).

8. Students should note the number of documents authored by women (five are cited as being by women). Some students will argue that women seemed to readily accept and promote a passive, subordinate role. Ask why women would accept such a role. Other students will emphasize the seeming manipulation and domination by men. Thus, women had little choice but to accept their subordinate role. Ask what evidence students have to support this claim.

9. Letters by women and diaries in which women talk about the virtues of the passive, subordinate role would support the statement in question 8. The more widespread, the more support it would give. What would students think if they found statements by Native American women of a subordinate role? These women never read the magazines and books listed here. This might indicate another factor in shaping the roles of men and women. Actually, in some tribes, women had central roles in decision making, for example in selecting the chief and controlling property.

Lesson 8: What Arguments Were Made for and against Women's Rights?

Objectives

To evaluate evidence
To make inferences
To identify the ad hominem fallacy
To identify the rhetorical question technique
To identify and evaluate value claims
To evaluate generalizations

Teaching Ideas

Begin by asking if anyone has ever heard of the Seneca Falls Convention. Instruct students to read the Declaration of Sentiments and Resolutions (Documents A and B) and answer the questions. Have them, in groups of three, discuss their answers. Discuss the answers as a class. Reactions to the Convention can be introduced by having students read Document C, and answering questions 7 and 8.

Part II is set up for a debate, but you could supplement or supplant it with an analysis of particular arguments. Have students fill in the chart on p. 70. One way to do argument analysis is to have each small group of students evaluate one or two arguments from a document and report its evaluation. Or students could answer questions 9–14, which focus on a few particular points. Another focus could be on the strategies of each side. Why do the prosuffrage people argue the points they do? What groups are the antisuffrage people trying to persuade?

Conclude this lesson by having students write a 100-word response to question 6, or draw a cartoon as it would have been drawn in 1920 for or against woman suffrage. (Cartoons use symbols and few words to make their points. Students should explain the meaning of the cartoon in 25 to 50 words on the back of the sheet.)

Suggested Answers

1. It was modeled after the Declaration of Independence to show that the ideals of 1776 had not been achieved. The purpose of this format was to show people who opposed the Declaration of Sentiments that they were opposing the same philosophy embodied in the Declaration of Independence.

2. Students will give a variety of answers which will reveal their assumptions about the importance of various rights.

3. At the time, most men and women would have been opposed to the Declaration of Sentiments and Resolutions. Ask students why. (Too radical a change from their conception of the proper role of women?) But this conclusion about why people opposed the Seneca Falls Sentiments and Resolution is deceptive because it tells us nothing about subgroups of men and women, such as poor vs. rich, blacks, Native Americans, and Hispanics. Students should evaluate the generalizations they make.

4. Students should be able to offer several arguments, such as: this is too radical; women aren't logical enough to vote intelligently; women should not be involved in business or owning property; equality in marriage is unbiblical. They will be interested to see that one argument (in Document C) is to attack the people who wrote the documents.

5. Several inferences you could make about the authors: they are literate; they are well educated; they believe that the system can be reformed; they believe that people can be persuaded through logical arguments; they believe in equal rights for women; they believe in natural rights; they believe in God.

6. Now this should get some interesting responses!

7. Make students support their views with examples.

8. Students should note several grievances that still exist.

9. This is the ad hominem (attacking the arguer) fallacy, described on page 14. This article tries to discredit the Declaration of Sentiments by making fun of the women who wrote it.

10. Students might suggest: fear of change; personalizing; a difference of viewpoints.

11. Students should be able to write five arguments for each side in the debate.

12. There are several interesting points about Document A by Franklin Collins:

   a. It is set up in rhetorical questions. Explain that rhetorical questions imply the answer (the point being made) without ever stating the point. To several of these questions, one could answer "no."

   b. Some evidence should be presented to support the

second question. ("Do a majority of the women of the United States want the ballot?")

   c. The author makes the argument that woman suffrage in four western states has not purified politics, so it should be opposed at the national level. But suffragists were arguing, at least in part, that women should be able to vote as a right, not because they would purify politics. American Revolutionaries argued for independence as a right, not because they thought they could purify American government.

13. The authors of B use the ad hominem technique when they ask why every socialist supports suffrage.

14. The Catholic clergymen base their arguments on assumptions about women and their proper role in society. If the assumptions are wrong, their arguments collapse. Several assumptions are made: women are gentle, tender, etc.; women are queens of the household—that's where they need to be; men's role in the home is not as important (or necessary) as women's role.

15. Antisuffragists were appealing to Catholics; working women and men; antiradicals; men in general (fear of losing status); and women in general ("Do you want to have to serve in the military?")

16. Document H is appealing to traditional women in the roles of mother.

17. Note that Caroline Lowe, like Franklin Collins, uses the rhetorical question (see answer 9). Her point about the teachers not having pay restored due to lack of a vote is a strong one, but there might have been other causes for not restoring pay.

18. The 100 vilest men in the state having more power in the legislature than the suffragists is interesting, but no evidence is presented to support the claim.

Lesson 9: Was Andrew Jackson a Representative of the Common People?

Objectives

To find the main idea
To identify and evaluate evidence
To identify and evaluate generalizations
To identify and evaluate cause and effect
To identify and evaluate debating reasoning
To recognize unstated assumptions

Teaching Ideas

The recommended way of teaching this lesson is to have students read both viewpoints and answer the questions. Discuss their answers. At this point you could end the lesson or have students research the topic to find evidence supporting either Historian A or Historian B. That is, were Jackson and the Democrats mainly supported by the common people, while the rich mainly supported the Whigs?

Other methods could be used, such as ARMEAR analysis or a debate, but these methods may not be too effective due to the brevity of the interpretations.

Suggested Answers
Historian A

1. The main point is that Andrew Jackson was the representative of and promoted the interests of the common people.

2. The argument in the first paragraph, second sentence is a generalization. The sample size is not given, but it looks like no sample was used at all. Rather, it looks like the author inferred that if "the rich" benefited from these policies, they must have pushed the policies. The other weakness in the argument is the term "rich." Do the rich really operate as a group? Some people believe they do, while others believe they don't.

3. This argument uses cause-and-effect reasoning. The Whigs used mass rallies and avoiding the issues (causes) to get elected (effect) in 1840. There is a reasonable connection between rallies and election voting, but it isn't very strong. Many other factors, such as ethnic group affiliation and strength of the economy, might be more influential in voting choice. Therefore, this cause-and-effect argument is rather weak.

4. There is no evidence presented in this interpretation. This makes it a very weak argument.

5. The author has a rather simplistic view of the political system in which most poor people were in the Democratic Party while most rich people were in the Whig Party. The author seems to see only heroes (Democrats/Jackson) and villains (Whigs), as he emphasizes the good points of the Democrats, even of the spoils system, while focusing only on the bad points of the Whigs. This is the fallacy of special pleading. The author is too partisan.

6. Based on the above comments, this is a very weak argument. It's simplistic and is not supported by evidence.

HISTORIAN B

7. The main point is that Historian A and other liberal historians are wrong—Andrew Jackson and the Democratic Party were not the representatives of the common man against the rich.

8. This is debating reasoning. It seems to be a fair criticism of Historian A's view, but we haven't seen the other liberal interpretations of the Jacksonian period, so we don't know if Historian B's charge is fair that the liberal view oversimplifies and distorts the time period. Maybe Historian B has put forth straw men (p. 14) to discredit, for example.

9. Historian B reasons by generalization in the third and fourth paragraphs. The sample within New York State, shown in endnote 1, is impressive since it covers all counties. One weakness is that it doesn't include urban areas. However, the sample is from only one state. Maybe Pennsylvania or Virginia had different voting patterns, with the poor mainly voting Democrat and the rich mainly voting Whig. This problem shows the need for regional studies to test generalizations made for the country as a whole.

10. The book by Lee Benson (endnote 1) is a secondary source. There is no apparent reason to lie and there are no corroborating sources. The research into voting patterns looks careful and scholarly.

11. This interpretation is much stronger than that by Historian A. The sample needs to be expanded to other states, but at least there is some evidence presented showing why people voted the way they did.

UNIT 3
SLAVERY

Lesson 10: Identifying and Evaluating Evidence

Objectives

To identify sources
To evaluate evidence

Teaching Ideas

This is a reinforcement lesson on skills from Lesson 1 and 2, so it need not take a lot of class time. If students answer the questions for homework, they can compare their answers in small groups and then discuss them as a class fairly quickly.

Suggested Answers

1. S   The *Chicago Herald* is the source.

2. N

3. S   Hinton Helper is the source.

4. N

5. N

6. S   The *Atlantic Monthly* article is the source.

7. N

8. Henry Wilson

STRENGTHS
- Wilson might be a trained historian, but we don't know that. Students may know other (O) evidence that supports his claim.

WEAKNESSES
- Wilson is a secondary source, has a reason to lie (R), and there is no other (O) evidence given here to support his claim.

9. Maria Perkins

STRENGTHS
- Maria is a primary (P) source, and it is hard to see why she would lie (R) to her husband about her feelings, since it is a private (P) letter.

WEAKNESSES
- There is no other (O) evidence supporting her claim. She is also emotionally upset, which might affect her perspective.

10. Slave suicides

STRENGTHS
- The slave is a primary (P) source. The observation that the whites guarded the ship shows the problem of suicides was not rare. However, the slave

may have thought the guarding was to prevent suicides, whereas, it may have been for some other reason.

WEAKNESSES
- The book is a public (P) source. Since it was written by a slave, it may be exaggerating (R) how bad slave ships were and how bad he felt at the time. There are no other (O) sources supporting his view.

11. Frederick Douglass

STRENGTHS
- Douglass is a primary (P) source, and he is an expert in the sense of how slavery on his plantation worked.

WEAKNESSES
- Douglass has a reason (R) to lie. He's an abolitionist, so he has great incentive to exaggerate the evils of slavery. His autobiography was published, so this excerpt is public (P). There are no other (O) sources here to support this account, but elsewhere there are many accounts describing the evils of slavery.

12. Sir Charles Lyell

STRENGTHS
- Lyell is probably a primary (P) source since his description implies that he visited the Georgia plantation. However, it was a visit—he didn't live on the plantation year round as did Frederick Douglass.

WEAKNESSES
- Lyell may not be consciously lying (R) but his upper-class frame of reference would influence him to analyze the situation from the perspective of owners, not slaves. Most of his information would have come from owners. This is a public (P) source, and there is no supporting evidence (O) here.

It is important to note that both the accounts of Frederick Douglass and Sir Charles Lyell might be entirely true. The Maryland plantation could have been terrible for slaves, while the Georgia plantation may have been quite humane. One must be very cautious not to generalize about slavery in the South from a few, or even many, accounts.

Another possibility is that Lyell was on the Georgia plantation during a slack season. Maybe in the busy season, slaves were overworked as they were on the Maryland plantation.

Lesson 11: Assessing Cause and Effect

Objectives

To identify cause and effect
To evaluate cause and effect

Teaching Ideas

Students can write their answers for the section on identifying cause and effect, and you can discuss their answers quickly as a class. The section on evaluating cause and effect is more difficult. You might want to do problem 8 as a class if you think students could use the guidance. However, they can often teach each other in small group work.

Suggested Answers

IDENTIFYING CAUSE AND EFFECT

1. N

2. N

3. C Cause—sunbathing; effects—tan and possible cancer

4. C Cause—whipping; effect—Jane ran away

5. C Cause—underground railroad; effect—more slaves escaped

6. C Cause—Liberty Party took votes from Whigs; effect—Democrats won

7. N

EVALUATING CAUSE AND EFFECT

8. Garrison—There is a logical connection between criticism and getting upset, but not necessarily between criticism and hostility to abolitionism. Other factors besides Garrison's writing may have caused Northerners to oppose abolitionism. They may have feared war, felt there were constitutional questions that needed to be looked at, or had a financial stake in the continuation of slavery.

9. Nat Turner—It's logical that slaveholders would tighten up after an insurrection, but more evidence should be presented showing that slaveholders were fearful, i.e., showing the connection between the rebellion and the laws. This argument is in the form of the *post hoc* (after, therefore because of) fallacy (p. 6). Another possible cause for slaveholders tightening up is the rise of abolitionist activity in the North in the early 1830s. For example, the radical abolitionist newspaper, *The Liberator*, was established in 1831.

Lesson 12: Analyzing Generalizations

Objectives

To identify generalizations
To evaluate generalizations

Teaching Ideas

Students can write their answers for the section on identifying generalizations, and you can discuss their answers quickly as a class. The section on evaluating generalizations is more difficult. It might be best to do problem 8 as a class, and then have students do the rest of the problems. It is important to stress that students consider the subgroups of the whole population in evaluating generalizations.

Suggested Answers

IDENTIFYING GENERALIZATIONS

1. G "People" indicates a statement about a group.

2. G "Most" is the cue word.

3. N

4. G "Slaves" are a group.

5. G Statistics are information about groups.

6. N

7. G "Southerners" are a group.

EVALUATING GENERALIZATIONS

8. Slaves worked hard

The sample of 33 plantations is quite small to use to generalize about the whole South over a long period of time. There is no indication, moreover, that the sample is representative. All 33 estates could have been in one state and for rice plantations having over 100 slaves, all of which would be unrepresentative of the South. Note that this argument is an endnote for Historian C in Lesson 16.

9. States outlawed reading

Since there were only 11 Southern states it would have been easy to check all of them for laws against teaching slaves to read. Thus the argument may be representative. We don't know if the person making the claim actually checked the records. Another problem with the argument is in the language. How many states passed these laws?

10. Birth records

Since this historian did not generalize beyond that

single plantation, he has a strong conclusion. Birth records are likely to include all slaves, so the sample is of every slave on the plantation. Another strength is that the records are for 100 years, so it is a representative sample over time. We'd start having problems if we generalized this conclusion to South Carolina or the South.

11. Census of 1860

The author of this argument takes pains to show that these three states accurately represent the situation of slaves on cotton plantations in general, because these states produced such a large amount of cotton (almost half). While these three states had one-third of the South's slaves, the counties surveyed were only half the counties in the states. The number of slaves in the sample was only 4200 out of approximately 4 million slaves in 1860, or .1%, which is a very small sample. In addition, field hands may have had a higher mortality, which would make them overrepresented in the census under deaths. Even if the census were correct for 1860, moreover, it is not justified to generalize from it for cotton plantations through the whole antebellum period. Nevertheless, this is a much stronger sample than many made about slavery. At least the author tried to make it representative.

It might be interesting to compare the implication of problem 11 (slaves had little incentive to work hard) with the argument in problem 8 that slaves had incentive to work hard. Ask which generalization seems stronger. The one in problem 11 seems stronger, since we know the sample was spread out over three states and the generalization is only for cotton plantations, not all types of plantations.

Lesson 13: Identifying and Assessing Types of Reasoning

Objectives

To identify and evaluate cause and effect
To identify and evaluate generalizations
To identify and evaluate comparisons

Teaching Ideas

Have students fill in the answers individually and share their answers in small groups. Discuss their answers as a class. Some items could have several answers, so listen to the reasoning behind student answers.

Suggested Answers

1. New jeans

TYPE
- Cause and effect

EVALUATION
- The connection between not washing his new jeans (the cause) and having to wear his old jeans (effect) is clear, but only if he has but two pairs of jeans or hadn't washed other jeans, or has other pairs of slacks but prefers to wear only jeans. These other factors are also possible causes for having to wear his old jeans.

2. Internal improvement

TYPE
- Cause and effect; generalization

EVALUATION
- It does not necessarily follow that government involvement in a state in one way would lead to interference in another way. Southerners may have feared it, but the reason (connection) isn't compelling and no evidence of the fear is presented. Southerners may have opposed internal improvements for other reasons (other causes); for example, they may not have wanted their taxes to go up to pay for improvements.

3. Not all slaves treated badly

TYPE
- Generalization

EVALUATION
- No information is given about the size or representativeness of the sample. We don't know how many plantations or what records were examined.

4. High price for slavery

TYPE
- Cause and effect; generalization

EVALUATION
- The connection isn't quite clear. Why couldn't slaves have been used in industry or commerce?

The argument doesn't explain why slavery caused the South to remain agricultural (such as comparative advantage in agriculture; social/lifestyle choices) which should be examined.

5. Everyone affected

TYPE

*   Generalization

EVALUATION

*   No information is given on the size or representativeness of the sample. There probably wasn't a sample done. Rather, the claim likely is based on the inference that slavery must have affected everyone in the South.

6. Tobacco plantations

TYPE

*   Comparison

EVALUATION

*   Some possible differences between Kentucky and Missouri on the one hand and Virginia and Maryland on the other hand are climate, organization, and transportation. These factors should be explored to strengthen the comparison.

7. Slaves becoming Christians

TYPE

*   Cause and effect (motives are causes of behavior)

EVALUATION

*   These causes make sense (connections), but slaves may also have seemed to become believing Christians to avoid punishment or curry the favor of the owners.

8. White workers

TYPE

*   Generalization (It isn't cause and effect because no cause or reason is given for not wanting to work alongside blacks.)

EVALUATION

*   Again, we don't know how many white workers were sampled. Where would information about attitudes have been recorded? One source for the attitudes toward blacks might have been periodical articles, but those articles wouldn't necessarily represent the majority of white workers. The generalization is very weak.

Lesson 14: Was Slavery Good or Bad?

Objectives

To find the main idea
To identify and evaluate evidence
To identify fallacies
To evaluate generalizations

Teaching Ideas

Begin by asking half the students to role-play plantation owners in the South before the Civil War. They are to write a defense of slavery of 1 to 2 paragraphs. Have them read their arguments. Ask if they would really believe their arguments. There should be some disagreement. Some students may say they believe the arguments, while others may say they have convinced themselves to believe the arguments.

The other half of the class is to role-play slaves and write 1 to 2 paragraphs criticizing slavery. Would they really believe their arguments? Would slaves be more likely to believe the arguments they make against slavery than owners would be likely to believe the arguments they make to defend slavery?

Now have students read the two viewpoints and answer the questions. Discuss their answers.

Suggested Answers
VIEWPOINT A

1. Main point—Slavery is good for Negroes. (*Negro* is used in this analysis because that is the term used in the viewpoint.)

2. Fallacies—This is a list of some of the fallacies in the viewpoint.

   a. First sentence, first paragraph—Hasty generalization: <u>all</u> countries in <u>all</u> ages?

   b. Third sentence, first paragraph—Prevalent proof: "It is clear" is like saying "everyone knows."

   c. Fourth sentence, first paragraph—Stereotypes Negroes

   d. Second paragraph, first sentence—Stereotypes Negroes

   e. Second paragraph, second sentence—False scenario: We don't know if the Negro would be an insufferable burden since it hasn't happened yet.

   f. Second paragraph, third sentence—Either/or:

Rephrased this is "Either we enslave Negroes or they will become insufferable burdens on society." Actually, we could pass laws requiring all adults to save for retirement or a host of other possible solutions.

g. Third paragraph—Stereotyping Negroes and false scenario: "They would be far outstripped...."

h. Fourth paragraph, first sentence—Hasty generalization about the whole continent of Africa; special pleading in mentioning only the supposed good points of slavery without mentioning the bad points.

i. Fourth paragraph, second sentence—Special pleading: he may be pulling out the worst point of the North to characterize the area.

j. Fourth paragraph, last sentence—Special pleading that because Negro men do not kill Negro women, their moral condition is better in slavery (though their women are sexually abused by owners, both men and women are whipped, and so forth).

3. There is no evidence presented in this viewpoint.

4. Initially students may say that Fitzhugh was rationalizing something which he knew was wrong. Eventually someone may say that Fitzhugh might have believed everything he wrote. It might be interesting to discuss how he could believe these things. Did most people in the South believe them? How could people come to believe these things?

5. The key assumption in this argument is that slavery is close to family as a system. A counterargument is that some owners whipped and overworked slaves and divided families in order to make money, which seems more like capitalism than family. Only in the dark side of family life—incest, wife beatings, and neglect—does slavery on some plantations resemble family.

VIEWPOINT B

6. Main point—Slavery is wrong.

7. Reasoning

a. Generalization—The author says a thousand witnesses from newspaper ads. This is a significant sample showing a certain level of brutality. But ads were for runaways who were more likely to be whipped (which is why they ran away sometimes). So it is not representative of all slavery.

b. Proof by evidence or example and generalization—The strength of the proof is dependent on the evidence or examples.

8. This is the prevalent proof fallacy ("everybody knows").

9. All of the sources are primary and have no reason to lie. They are what historians call "innocent." That is, they were written for one purpose (recovering lost slaves) but used by the author to prove something else (slaves were mistreated). This "innocence" makes the sources reliable.

10. As mentioned in the answer to 7a, if all thousand witnesses are reliable then a certain level of violence is established regarding slavery. The question is, What level? Do the thousand witnesses represent thousands of others who have been brutalized or are they the exception, pulled out by the abolitionist author to exaggerate his case?

Lesson 15: How Did Slavery Affect Slaves?

Objectives

To identify and evaluate evidence
To identify and evaluate cause and effect
To identify and evaluate generalizations
To identify and evaluate comparisons
To use relevant information to evaluate arguments

Teaching Ideas

This lesson and Lesson 16 are basically the same. There are three interpretations in Lesson 16 (as opposed to two in this lesson), and the interpretations are much longer and more complex in Lesson 16. You can choose which readings to give your students. If you have heterogenous classes, you could give some students the interpretations from this lesson and other students the interpretations from Lesson 16. The lesson plans are essentially the same except as noted in the lesson plan for Lesson 16.

Begin the lesson by reading the excerpts from *Uncle Tom's Cabin* (pp. 98–99) and *Gone with the Wind* (p. 99). Ask students what impression these readings give of slavery. Why do the impressions differ so much? How could we check on these sources further? How reliable are novels as historical sources? Introduce for consideration the difference in expectations for a novel and an historical work. The test of excellence for novels is, Could it have happened this way? Historical works are subject to a different question: <u>Did</u> it happen this way? As such, historical works must meet standards of excellence in the use and interpretation of evidence. If a historical novel influences our views about history, shouldn't it be subject to standards of historical criticism, apart from literary standards? This issue of how to evaluate historical novels is dealt with again in Book 3 of this series, *Reconstruction to Progressivism*, Lesson 17 on *The Jungle*.

Students should now read the interpretations on slavery. The class can read Historian A, analyze it and discuss it, then repeat the process for Historian B. Or students can read both viewpoints and evaluate them at the same time. Or half the class could be asked to evaluate Historian A while the other half evaluates Historian B. Remind students to look at the relevant information.

Students could be asked to evaluate the viewpoints according to the ARMEAR Model (p. 18 in the student book) or by the worksheet in this lesson. A third option is to have students read both viewpoints and decide which viewpoint is stronger. Have students explain in writing two strengths of the viewpoint they select and two weaknesses of the other viewpoint. The class could then debate the topic. Of course, the lesson will be adapted for the particular needs of your students. Perhaps you will want to focus on only one or two skills, such as evaluating evidence or comparisons. Focusing on fewer skills will shorten the lesson, which is always a consideration in history courses.

Suggested Answers
HISTORIAN A

1. Main point: Slavery in the United States was very bad, crushing the personalities of slaves.

2. Evidence

   a. Endnote 1—Since it was published before slavery ended, we could assume the author checked the laws in the Southern states. However, the laws themselves are the primary sources, so this book is secondary (P). The author has an obvious reason to lie (R), being published by an anti-slavery society. There is no corroboration (O), but it could be checked.

   b. Endnote 3—This is a secondary source (P) which is very weak for this key point.

3. Reasoning, second paragraph: This is a comparison. One could argue that in terms of the one essential characteristic, control, slavery was like a concentration camp; however, the differences are substantial and seem to undermine the comparison argument. Students should look at the relevant information. Numbers 1–5 and 11, especially 4 and 11, show that concentration camp prisoners would have been controlled to a greater extent than would slaves. Prisoners were killed regularly whereas slaves were not. So slave owners would have to compromise in some situations. (Why kill or injure a slave for a minor offense?) There were much greater limits to slave owner's control. Essentially, slavery was a labor system whereas concentration camps were for killing.

4. Cause-and-effect reasoning, second and third paragraphs: The author is arguing that owner control caused slaves to have passive personalities. The connection makes sense—when a person is under the control of another, he or she may become very passive. (It may also cause the person to become rebellious, but the connection is nevertheless plausible.) However, there are numerous possible causes for a slave to act

passive other than having a passive, give-up-the-fight personality. The most likely cause is passive resistance. That is, slaves may have been passive and docile to get out of work or at least slow down the pace. This is a far different passive behavior than in concentration camps. Slaves may have been passive, in other words, as an expression of an active choice to control their work situation, whereas concentration camp inmates may have been crushed psychologically.

5. Overall, Historian A's interpretation is quite weak. It is based on weak sources. Historian A never really proved the widespread existence of the passive personality (which is key to the interpretation) since the claim is based on only one weak secondary source. Even if slaves did act passively, however, we cannot conclude, as Historian A does, that their personalities were crushed by slavery. As we have seen above, passive behavior may actually have been active resistance.

   The analogy to concentration camps is also weak due to the significant differences between slavery (a system of labor) and concentration camps (primarily for death).

HISTORIAN B

6. Main point: Generally, slaves were treated well by their masters.

7. Endnote 1—What's missing is the source of the numbers. Presumably, Historian B looked at plantation records, totalled up food intake, and calculated nutritional values. We'd like to know which plantations, how many, where they were located, and from what years the data was compiled.

8. Fallacy in second paragraph: Numbers fallacy ("I'm right because I have more facts.")

9. Comparison in paragraph 3: The comparison is weak in a number of ways. First, urban housing tends to be smaller than rural housing. Second, this is for slum housing (endnote 2) which tends to be smaller still. Third, since when is the size of housing an indication of the quality of housing? Basically, the author is comparing the typical slave house to the smallest housing for free people (the fallacy of special pleading) and saying that because slave housing was larger, it was better. It's a weak argument.

10. Reasoning in paragraph 4: The author is generalizing

that slaves were not often whipped based on the records of only one plantation for only two years. This is a very small sample and is not likely to be representative of the whole South. Maybe most masters whipped more frequently than did Barrow.

There is a second problem also. A whipping is a brutal act of punishment, which could kill a slave. One public whipping per year to one slave on the whole plantation may therefore have been enough to terrify slaves and achieve a good deal of control. Eighty whippings per year was almost two per week! Far from showing a lack of physical punishment, these statistics paint a brutal picture of slavery. Some whippings were probably relatively minor, but even if 1 out of 10 was a serious beating, slaves would have seen a brutal whipping once a month. The second sentence in paragraph 4 is also interesting. Few historians argue that slave owners relied on the whip <u>alone</u>. So this is a straw man fallacy (p. 14).

11. Reasoning in paragraph 5: This is a comparison of output per year rather than the normal output per hour. (Relevant information #9) The South has a longer growing season (Relevant information #10) so slaves would have worked more hours per year. (They could have been forced to work more hours per day, also, since the slave owner controlled their schedules.) So, even if slaves were less efficient, producing less per hour, they could have produced more per year since they worked more hours.

   Second, greater efficiency may have been achieved because cotton gives a greater yield for each unit of labor. Third, plantations were larger on a whole than Northern farms so efficiency may have come from economies of scale rather than from slavery itself.

12. Reasoning in paragraph 6: This is a cause-and-effect argument. The argument is that freedom caused slaves to be worse off. This is probably true, but there are many other possible causes for slaves being worse off, such as the Civil War, the poor economy of the South at the time, the oppressive actions taken by some Southern whites against freedmen, or poor policies by the federal and state governments. However, even if freedmen were worse off entirely because they were freed from slavery, it does not prove that slavery wasn't that bad. It may actually show some of the debilitating effects of slavery on slaves.

13. Historian B's interpretation is riddled with problems, as shown above. The idea of using computers to study statistical information in history is worthwhile and will no doubt add to our understanding of the past. Unfortunately, this interpretation suffered from faulty assumptions, unrepresentative samples, weak cause-and-effect relationships, and false analogies. Computers are worthwhile tools but a standard saying holds true for them: Garbage in, garbage out.

Lesson 16: What Was It Like to Be a Slave?

Objectives

To identify and evaluate evidence
To identify and evaluate cause and effect
To identify and evaluate generalizations
To identify and evaluate comparisons
To use relevant information to evaluate arguments
To identify unstated assumptions

Teaching Ideas

As mentioned in the lesson plan for Lesson 15 (pp. 81–85), this lesson is longer and more complicated than Lesson 15, but otherwise these two lessons are basically the same. Therefore, use the teaching ideas outlined in Lesson 15 for ideas for this lesson.

As with Lesson 15, it is recommended that you begin the lesson by reading the excerpts from *Uncle Tom's Cabin* and *Gone with the Wind*. Before students begin reading the Historians' viewpoints, have them read "Comments on the Books" (pp. 119–20). Discuss whether comments from the book covers should sway us in reading or believing a book.

The lesson options for the interpretations themselves are outlined in Lesson 15. The answers included here are for the worksheet included in this lesson (pp. 121–27 in the student text). Remind students to look at the relevant information (pp. 118–19) in order to fully evaluate the viewpoints.

Suggested Answers

HISTORIAN A

1. Main point (possible answers)

   - Slavery in the United States was a brutal institution which crushed the personalities of slaves.

   - The closed system of slavery in the United States, with its complete power to the slave owner, caused the docile personalities among slaves.

2. Paragraph 2

   Reasoning: Comparison

   Question: Are the two cases sufficiently different (in this argument) to justify the conclusion that slavery was much worse in the United States?

   Evaluation: The relevant information (#17) shows that Latin American slavery was not so different (not so much more humane) from slavery in the United States. This is a weak comparison.

3. Paragraph 12

Students should recognize this as a comparison and question whether United States slavery is really similar to a concentration camp. The relevant information suggests one important difference—slavery was for labor, while concentration camps were for death. So slaves were not treated as cruelly.

4. Paragraph 8

Negative proof (p. 12 in the "Guide to Critical Thinking," Unit 1). The lack of evidence does point in the direction of no slaves with passive personalities, but we must be careful about accepting "a lack of evidence" for proof.

5. Sambo in paragraph 7

The key here is to look at the evidence in endnote 17. The evidence is a secondary source. We should insist on better evidence before we accept this argument.

Another way to evaluate the argument is by asking how good the sample is to support the generalization. We have no evidence that any sample was done. How many slaves actually exhibited the passive personality? This is a weak point in Historian A's case.

6. Evaluate evidence

Did the students evaluate it according to PROP or other specific criteria, or did they make some vague comments?

7. Overall evidence

Many of the sources are secondary. It might be a good idea to talk with students about how to figure out if evidence is primary or secondary. Tell them to look at endnote 4. How do they know if it is primary or secondary? (Look at date of publication.) Go into more detail (editor, reprint date, etc.) if necessary.

HISTORIAN B

8. Main point (possible answers)

- Historian A is wrong; slavery in the United States did not totally crush the personalities of slaves.

- Slavery in the United States was often cruel, but

slaves were able to resist it and maintain strong personalities and a sense of community.

9. E   Point out that this is something which historians do regularly.

10. Which statements support the view that slaves had minds of their own? (Put a check on the line.)

A. ✓   Supports the argument.

B. ✓   Supports the argument.

C. This is difficult to tell. Is frequent flogging a sign of a will to resist rules (as Historian B argues), or a sign of the total domination and brutality of slave owners? The author has not identified the cause of the whippings. This could be a post hoc fallacy (p. 6 in the "Guide").

D. No. The author is obligated to overcome this contrary evidence. This is dealt with in question 11.

11. There are many possible factors which could cause something to happen in one place (more slave revolts in Latin America) but not in another (fewer slave revolts in the United States). Unlike science, it is impossible to separate the factors in history and study them separately to prove which is the key factor. Moreover, Historian B does not give us any evidence that the low probability of success was the deciding factor in keeping down the number of revolts in the United States. He does not disprove the argument that slaves didn't revolt because of their passive personalities.

12. Reasoning in paragraph 14

Reasoning: Generalization

Question: How representative is the sample?

Evaluation: Though it is only six counties from three states, it might still be representative. Were the counties picked randomly? Otherwise, it might be special pleading (p. 11, "Guide"). The author does not tell us what the time period is for marriage certificates. If it is a short time period, the sample wouldn't be representative over time.

13. Most are primary sources. Explain to students how they can tell (see the answer for question 7).

14. Evaluate evidence (cue to use PROP, if necessary)

    A. Endnote 2

        P — Primary

        R — He might have reason to distort to make himself and his fellow slaves look better.

        O — No corroborating evidence

        P — Public, it's a book.

    B. Endnote 29

        P — Primary; the title indicates that the author had been a slave.

        R —He has a reason to lie. He is showing slave men as respected.

        O —No corroborating evidence

        P —Public

HISTORIAN C

15. Main point (possible answers)

- While slavery was evil in depriving slaves of their freedom, it generally treated slaves well.

- Other historians have been wrong in exaggerating the bad aspects of slavery. Slavery was not bad in its treatment of slaves.

16. E   "The accepted view..." indicates Historian C is going to show what is wrong with the accepted view.

17. Paragraph 3

    A. Debating

    B. Possible false assumptions. <u>Can</u> history be scientifically objective? Historians disagree on this question.

    C. Fallacy: Numbers (p. 12, "Guide")

18. It's a sample from only three plantations. We need more evidence than this to support the generalization that medical care was good throughout the entire South.

19. Assumption in paragraph 12

    The assumption is that all members of slave families

were owned by the same master. (If they were not owned by the same master, then movement of one master would break up the family.) (Relevant information 12)

20. The sample is too small. It is only one county to represent the whole South. Moreover, it only samples the years 1820 to 1840 to represent the whole time period from the start of slavery (1670) up to the Civil War.

21. Anne Arundel County is not a typical county. Many slaves sold out of this county would not have been recorded on the county records (but rather on the records of Washington and Baltimore). So the 1.92% slaves sales is probably too low. (Relevant information 13 and 14)

22. Paragraph 17

    Reasoning: Debating

    Question: Is it a fair attack on the other viewpoints?

    Evaluation: Straw Man fallacy. (Have students look this up in their "Guides," p. 14, if they didn't get it.) No evidence is presented that historians commonly believe all slaves were menial laborers. It's hard to believe any historians believed all slaves were menial laborers. Thus Historian C is debating an argument which opponents never made.

23. Endnote 14

    Did students look at the relevant information without any cue to do so? The problem is that this parish (county) is not typical. There might be a higher percentage of skilled workers because of the coopers. (Relevant information 15 and 16)

24. Paragraph 18

    There are at least two things which are possibly wrong:

    1. One plantation to represent the whole South is an unrepresentative sample.

    2. 0.7 whippings per slave per year may actually show extreme brutality. A slave on this plantation

may have seen more that 50 whippings per year. Considering that whippings could be fatal and were often public, they could send a brutal message.

25. Paragraph 20

    Reasoning: Comparison (analogy)

    Question: Are the two cases similar enough to justify the conclusion?

    Evaluation: They are not similar enough. The South has a longer growing season (output per *year* is not usually used to measure efficiency) and has more crops to select from to grow, so enjoys a comparative advantage. Moreover, slaves worked longer days than Northern farmers. (Relevant information 9, 10) So greater output was more likely due to climate and weather, not slaves' voluntary hard work or efficiency.

26. Attacking the Arguer (p. 14, "Guide")

OVERALL

27. Ask students to explain their reasons.

Lesson 17: What Do Visual Sources Show about Slavery?

Objectives

To evaluate evidence

Teaching Ideas

Ask students to write some words that come to mind when they think of slavery, and then write a sentence or two describing slavery around 1850. Discuss student responses. Where did they get their ideas?

One place people get their views of slavery is from visual sources. Have students read the introduction, examine the sources, fill in the chart, and answer the questions. They can then form small groups and share their responses. Discuss the sources as a class.

Suggested Answers

Answers to table shown on next page.

1. Student opinions will vary.

2. Possible answers: E is the most reliable; C is the least reliable—it isn't about slavery.

3. Student opinions will vary.

Source	What type of visual source is it?	What does it show about slavery?	How reliable is this source? (Consider at least 2 criteria.)
A	Lithograph	Peaceful, joyful, idyllic	The date indicates the picture was done after slavery had ended. As a drawing, it seems fanciful rather than realistic. It looks like a defense of slavery—a biased source. However, it may not be about slavery. It might be depicting life on plantations after the Civil War. The evidence doesn't clarify what it is showing.
B	Wood engraving from a sketch	Slavery is inhuman.	The sketch is probably a primary source. We don't know if Davis has a reason to lie—he might be an abolitionist.
C	Chromolithograph (a popular but less clear form of lithography)	It's hard to tell. The lack of movement gives a peaceful feeling, but the blacks don't look very happy either.	This visual is not about slavery! Did students note this from the information? Have students try to find it in textbooks to illustrate the section on slavery.
D	Lithograph	It seems to show slavery as hard work but the living conditions as not too bad.	The captions show it to be done for some religious purpose, probably making slaves more accepting of slavery. The drawing seems to make a general point rather than a specific scene. It's not meant to be realistic.
E	Photograph	It is brutal. It gives a very different impression from Source A, for example.	This source is the most reliable because it is a photo. Nevertheless, the person who took the picture had a motive. Maybe this slave was picked out because of his brutal story. Also, the slave does say the overseer was dismissed which shows some owners did not agree with this level of brutality.
F	Painting	Slavery is hard work.	A painting is less reliable than a photograph. Without any date or information on the artist, it is difficult to judge beyond the general weakness of a painting.
G	Woodcut from a sketch	Slaves sometimes enjoyed themselves.	The person who did the sketch is racially prejudiced against blacks. The physical characteristics of blacks, such as eyes, lips, and hair, are exaggerated, reinforcing the "Sambo" (happy slave) stereotype of blacks. The caption, "Sing, Darkeys, Sing," reinforces the racist tone. This is a very biased, impressionistic, rather than realistic, view of what some slave owners may have imagined slavery was like.

Lesson 18: Were Slaves Fed an Adequate Diet?

Objectives

To find the main idea
To evaluate proof by eliminating alternative reasoning
To evaluate generalizations
To evaluate evidence
To evaluate cause and effect
To relate hypotheses to relevant information

Teaching Ideas

Begin by asking students what "well fed" means. What is an adequate diet? Can you be well fed in terms of calories but not nutrients? How do we measure nutrient adequacy? (Recommended Daily Allowances) Can you eat the right foods but still have vitamin and mineral deficiencies? (Yes, if you don't properly absorb the nutrients, or if you have some illness that depletes your nutrients.) Were slaves well fed? Make sure students understand *Recommended Daily Allowance* before proceeding with the lesson.

Now have students read the overview, relevant information, and Parts I–III, and then answer questions 1–4. Discuss their answers. Next have students read Parts IV and V and answer questions 5–6. Discuss those answers, and have students read Parts VI and VII and answer questions 7–8. Discuss their answers, and discuss students' answers to the general questions (9–14).

You could also have students read all the viewpoints and answer all the questions in one assignment. Or you could have students read the viewpoints without answering the questions and discuss the general question: Were slaves fed an adequate diet?

Suggested Answers

1. One strength of this interpretation is that four historians from different time periods agree that slaves were fed a monotonous diet. Of course, Historians B, C, and D could have obtained their idea from Historian A without having established the slave diet by independent research. Also, no evidence is presented to support this claim.

2. Historian E attacks Historians A–D for claiming slaves were not well fed. The problem is Historian E changed the meaning of "well fed." Whereas Historians A–D argued that slaves got enough calories but were not well fed nutritionally, Historian E says the

other historians are wrong to say slaves were not well fed—in terms of calories. Historian E has criticized a straw man (p. 14).

3. The mention of food in plantation records does not mean it was eaten by slaves. This argument, by itself, is weak.

4. One possible weakness in this line of reasoning (proof by eliminating alternatives) is if all the alternatives have not been eliminated; for example, what if there was a great deal of spoilage? Other than spoilage, it is hard to think what else could have happened to the food, so maybe this is a good argument. The argument is also based on a generalization, which will be evaluated in question 8.

5. The criticisms could be very significant, but we don't know for sure. The mention of foods was already discussed in question 3. The difference in conversion tables would overestimate meat consumption, but we don't know by how much. The plantation sample may not be representative but, again, we don't know. If slaves were better fed on large plantations, then Historians F and G have an unrepresentative sample. The fourth criticism about other foods fed to animals is hard to judge, since Historian H has only a few responses to a questionnaire to support his claim. More evidence needs to be presented on this point.

6. Historians F and G have defended their original interpretation very well. The argument in paragraph 4, that even Historian H's revised diet is nutritionally adequate, is significant. The argument in paragraph 5 is also important that slaves ate foods not listed in plantation records. One weakness of the evidence is it was made 65 years after the events, but there doesn't seem to be a reason to lie.

7. Historians I and J use cause-and-effect reasoning. More specifically, they found certain effects (nutritional diseases) and reason that therefore certain causes (nutritional deficiencies) must have been present. Note that this is an interesting new angle from which to study the topic (effect to cause).

Unfortunately, the relevant information shows that the diseases cannot be attributed to what slaves were fed alone. Slaves had physical problems which caused two of the deficiencies. Lactose intolerance and black pigmentation (#5 b, c) would lead to vitamin D and calcium deficiencies reducing absorption of other nutrients even if they ate the perfect American Dietetic Association diet. Relevant information #8 shows slaves got enough magnesium and #12 and #13 show they probably have taken in enough iron (See Part V, paragraph 5 on molasses consumption). Thus, while slaves suffered nutritional diseases, it wasn't due to what they were fed. The argument about pica is quite interesting but, again, it might be due to malabsorption of minerals due to lack of vitamin D and calcium due to physical problems.

One interesting question that students could research is whether blacks in Africa also suffered the nutritional diseases outlined by Historians I and J.

8. Historians K, L, and M have a much smaller generalization (2 states over 60 years, rather than 11 states over almost 200 years) than do the other historians. This makes the conclusion more reliable within these two states. More state studies need to be done to improve the overall generalization.

9. Most students should believe that slaves were adequately fed in terms of calories.

10. The arguments that slaves received a nutritional diet seem stronger than the opposing view. However, students should be much less certain of their conclusion to this question than in #9, where there is more consensus among historians.

11. A wide variety of skills and expert knowledge were required: research skills; skills in asking questions, making inferences, drawing conclusions, and so forth; knowledge of medicine (diseases), nutrition, conversion of food production, types of crops and animals, climate, archaeology, statistics and mathematical formulas, the South and plantation life, farming, and African culture.

12. One possible reason is the topic is so complex that several experts have to work together to adequately interpret the information. Also, group discussions bring up a variety of perspectives. Many occupations are moving toward group investigation, which is why group work is done more frequently in school these days.

13. This is a matter of student opinion. On the topic of calories we seem to have a consensus. More research

may change our view of the nutritional adequacy of the slave diet.

14. The standards of excellence shown in this debate are on sample size and representativeness, adequateness of causal relationships and alternative causes, and adequateness of evidence. The standards are "enforced" by other historians, who write criticisms of the weak points (points that don't measure up to the standards of excellence) of interpretations.

UNIT 4
CIVIL WAR

Lesson 19: Assessing the Reliability of Sources

Objectives

To evaluate evidence

Teaching Ideas

This is a reinforcement lesson on evaluating evidence. (See Lessons 2 and 10.) Students fill in the strengths and weaknesses, then you can discuss them as a class. The discussion should go fairly quickly, but there are likely to be some disagreements and gray areas. Focus on the process, not right answers.

Suggested Answers

1. Slavery—*Uncle Tom's Cabin*

   STRENGTHS

   - Stowe took the stories in the novel from slave narratives and testimony.

   WEAKNESSES

   - Though it was written at the time (1852), it is not a primary source (P). Worse, it is a novel, so it doesn't have to be based on what really happened, but rather on whether it is believable. It could be totally inaccurate.

   - Stowe, as a Northerner, has a reason to lie (R) or exaggerate. Students might infer that she was an abolitionist.

   - This is a public source (P) and is meant to persuade people.

   - There is no other (O) evidence here showing slavery as evil.

2. Abraham Lincoln—Statement by Senator Douglas

   STRENGTHS

   - Douglas is a primary source (P) in the sense of being involved in the events and in knowing Lincoln. He may not, however, have heard Lincoln's House Divided speech, in which case he would be a secondary source.

   WEAKNESSES

   - Douglas has a reason to lie (R) in debate.

   - There is no other (O) evidence presented to support Douglas's claim.

- This is a public (P) debate in which both Lincoln and Douglas are trying to persuade the audience.

3. Secession—Trenton *Gazette*

STRENGTHS

- None

WEAKNESSES

- This is not a primary source (P); it has a reason to lie (R) being from the North and being public (P); and there is no other (O) evidence presented that it was a conspiracy.

4. Secession—Jefferson Davis

STRENGTHS

- Primary source (P)

WEAKNESSES

- Jefferson Davis has a reason to lie (R) to blame the war on the North; there is no other (O) evidence presented that the North caused secession; and this is a public (P) statement.

5. Secession—Randall

STRENGTHS

- While it may at first seem like he doesn't have a reason to lie (R), Randall may actually be distorting what he sees. In 1940 many Americans dreaded the possibility of war, so it is natural to look back and see other wars as unnecessary blunders. So, this could actually be a weakness.

WEAKNESSES

- This is a secondary source (P); no other (O) evidence is presented; and it is a public (P) article.

Lesson 20: Analyzing Cause and Effect

Objectives

To identify and evaluate cause-and-effect reasoning

Teaching Ideas

Have students read the introduction and, if necessary, ask questions to make sure they understand the relationship of the Kansas-Nebraska Act to the Missouri Compromise. Have them read the three viewpoints and explain under question 1 which viewpoint is strongest. Then have them discuss their answers in small groups and as a class. This lesson can serve as an introduction to more in-depth analyses of what constitutes a strong causal explanation. Students could be assigned to read several explanations of an event and required to write an evaluation of which explanation is best.

The section on identifying cause-and-effect arguments (questions 2–7) is meant to be a quick follow-up lesson. Have students answer the questions in this section and discuss as a class.

Suggested Answers

CONNECTION

1. Strongest viewpoint

   Based on the criterion of connecting the Kansas-Nebraska Act (the proposed cause) to the formation of the Republican Party (the effect), the best answer is Historian C. This viewpoint connects the Kansas-Nebraska Act to protest rallies and the meeting to form the Republican Party. It also shows that one of the planks in the Republican Party platform called for the repeal of the Kansas-Nebraska Act, and that in the same year following the passage of the Act, the newly-formed Republican Party had more members in Congress than did the Democrats. The election defeat of northern Democrats who voted for the Kansas-Nebraska Act further ties public anger with the existing party (and thus the need for a new party) to the rise of the Republicans.

   Historian A concentrates four of the five sentences on what caused the passage of the Kansas-Nebraska Act. Only the last sentence argues that the Act led to the formation of the Republican Party. The connection makes sense, but there is no evidence provided to show that Northerners were so upset that they would vote against traditional congressmen to support a new party. Nor is there evidence that the Republicans formed mainly to oppose the Act.

Historian B concentrates on the reasons why the Act was passed and the resulting violence. This historian connects the Republican Party to the opposition of the extension of slavery in the territories, but Historian C uses an actual plank from the Republican platform to make this connection more clearly. The Republicans winning 114 electoral votes shows strength, but that was two years later; there may have been reasons other than opposition to the Kansas-Nebraska Act which account for their strength. The results of the 1854 election, mentioned by Historian C, are much better evidence of Republican strength arising from anger over the Kansas-Nebraska Act.

IDENTIFYING CAUSE-AND-
EFFECT ARGUMENTS

2. C   Cause—CVS Pharmacy opened across the street; effect— local drugstore losing business

3. N   No cause for car ownership is proposed.

4. C   Cause—*Uncle Tom's Cabin*; effect—many Northerners hate slavery

5. N   No cause or effect is proposed for Douglas's accusation.

6. N   No cause or effect is proposed for the massacre.

7. C   Cause—"Dred Scott" decision; effect—controversy in the United States; antislavery Northerners upset

Lesson 21: Identifying and Evaluating Types of Reasoning

Objectives

To identify and evaluate cause and effect
To identify and evaluate generalizations
To identify and evaluate comparisons

Teaching Ideas

Have students fill in the answers individually, and then share their answers in small groups where they can help one another. Discuss their answers as a class. Since there are several types of reasoning possible for some items, listen for the reasons behind student answers.

Suggested Answers

1. North and West

TYPE OF REASONING

• Cause and effect, generalization

EVALUATION

• It is reasonable that transportation links would draw two regions together, so the connection is clear. However, the two regions may also have been drawn together because of emigration from North to West, or similarity of beliefs on political and other issues. It may be that similar beliefs or complimentary economic systems set the stage (partly caused) the building of railroads and canals, rather than the other way around.

2. 1840 election

TYPE OF REASONING

• Comparison, generalization

EVALUATION

• Slavery in 1840 and abortion today are similar in that they are both volatile, emotional issues. They both could cost politicians votes with a direct answer, and they both involve practices already taking place that some people are trying to stop. They are different in that slavery was much more of a regional issue—abortion is fought more often within states and is practiced nationwide, not just in the South.

3. Polk wins 1844 election

TYPE OF REASONING

• Cause and effect, generalization

EVALUATION

• If the Liberty Party did, in fact, take votes from Clay, then the connection is very clear. But there is no explanation of how this person knows the Liberty Party took more votes from Clay than from

Polk. Maybe the Liberty Party actually made the election closer. There are other possible causes for Clay losing the election, such as poor campaign techniques, lack of funding, past political performance, and the public's perception of him as a leader.

4. Liberty Party

TYPE OF REASONING
  • Generalization

EVALUATION
  • Vote counts are of all the votes cast, so they are complete rather than samples. Therefore, this statement is likely to be quite accurate.

5. Rivers in the South

TYPE OF REASONING
  • Cause and effect, generalization

EVALUATION
  • There is a connection between having convenient, natural, low-cost transportation available and deciding not to spend money to build other transportation lines. There are other reasons why the South may not have built railroads, however. For example, maybe Southerners wanted to preserve their slow-moving, easygoing life-style (their perception) and felt railroads would disrupt it too much.

6. Panic of 1857

TYPE OF REASONING
  • Cause and effect, generalization

EVALUATION
  • This is a tricky problem. The cause is the Panic, and the effect is Northern perception of a Southern conspiracy. (Your students may say the low tariff caused the Panic. But this argument talks only about Northern views of the South as a result of the Panic.) It is reasonable that Northerners might blame the depression on the South. There are, however, a number of other causes for Northerners not to like the South, for example, the debate over slavery.

7. Per capita income

TYPE OF REASONING
  • Comparison

EVALUATION
  • Prices may have been higher in the North, which would be a very important difference. This is why <u>real</u> per capita income is a more accurate measurement. Also, income in the South, while lower, may actually have been rising faster than in the North, which would change the picture somewhat. This

increase in Southern income is what was happening, according to one historian.

8. John Brown's raid

TYPE OF REASONING

- Cause and effect, generalization

EVALUATION

- The connection between John Brown's raid and the lack of compromise is explained, although it could be explained in more detail. There are other events, such as the Kansas-Nebraska Act, *Uncle Tom's Cabin*, and the gag rule, which may also have caused a lack of compromise.

9. Railroad track

TYPE OF REASONING

- Comparison

EVALUATION

- Maybe the South also had only 30% of the land area or 30% of the people. It may have been more difficult to build railroads in the South. Maybe alternative modes of transportation were more available in the South, making railroads less popular, but not due to a backward agricultural economy. There are significant possible differences.

10. Abolitionists

TYPE OF REASONING

- Generalization

EVALUATION

- We don't have any idea about how large or representative the sample is. It could be quite impressionistic, based on biographical information of a few abolitionists, or it could be quite extensive and representative.

Lesson 22: Identifying and Evaluating Proof and Debating Reasoning

Objectives

To identify and evaluate proof by evidence or example
To identify and evaluate proof by authority
To identify and evaluate debating or eliminating alternatives

Teaching Ideas

This is a straightforward lesson on practicing evaluating proof and debating reasoning. Make sure students read over the explanations on pages 11–14 of the student book before beginning the problems. They should note especially the cue words, questions to ask, and fallacies. Have them answer the questions, compare answers in small groups, and discuss their answers as a class. If necessary, do the first problem or two as a class, then have the students fill in the rest of the sheet on their own.

Suggested Answers

1. D   This is eliminating alternatives. If Candice was at the dance all evening, then she probably didn't walk the dog. But she could have done it before or after the dance.

2. A   The leading theatre critic should carry some weight, but art is pretty subjective. We may not like something the critic thought was great. Besides, who says this critic is the leading one in the United States?

3. E   The example does help prove the point.

4. A   The historian's reputation as a respected authority does lend his argument more consideration, but the main test is the argument and evidence themselves. Who says the historian is respected?

5. D   This is a fair criticism of the previous historian in the sense that the writer criticized the argument rather than the person. We don't know, based on these brief summaries, which historian has the better argument.

6. E/A The *Congressional Record* is an authoritative source which provides good evidence to support the statement. The record could also be checked easily, which makes it even more reliable.

7. E   It's in the evidence category, even though there is no evidence. The argument is saying that there

is so much evidence that everyone knows it's true. This is the prevalent proof ("everyone knows") fallacy, student book, page 12.

8. E The photographs provide evidence that the Civil War was horrible.

9. D The problem here is all the Union generals have not been eliminated. What about Generals Sherman or Sheridan?

10. E This is the numbers fallacy, page 12.

Lesson 23: Which Side Caused the Firing on Fort Sumter?

Objectives

To find the main idea
To identify the Either-or fallacy
To identify the False Scenario fallacy

Teaching Ideas

This is intended to be a short lesson on identifying main points and fallacies. Have students fill in the answers individually, share their answers in small groups, and discuss as a class. You can shorten the lesson by skipping the small group step.

Suggested Answers
VIEWPOINT A

1. Possible main points:

   • Lincoln used Fort Sumter to get the Confederates to fire first.

   • The Confederates had no choice but to attack Fort Sumter.

2. D According to Viewpoint A, either the South could have attacked the Fort or backed down. Actually, as is pointed out in Viewpoint B, maybe the Confederates could have stopped the supply ships. Or perhaps they could have negotiated. The point is that the two alternatives given in the argument may not have been the only possible ones.

VIEWPOINT B

3. Possible main points:

   • The Confederates chose war by attacking Fort Sumter.

   • Lincoln did not maneuver the Confederates into attacking Fort Sumter.

4. B We have no way of knowing whether the Southerners would have demanded Fort Pickens. The author should give us some evidence to support the claim. Without any evidence the claim is guesswork, since it didn't happen.

5. Both viewpoints are very weak. Student answers may reveal unstated assumptions about the North and South in 1861.

Lesson 24: What Do Historians Assume about the Causes of War?

Objectives

To identify unstated assumptions

Teaching Ideas

This lesson is divided into four parts, so the teacher can choose one or two parts to fit a particular goal without taking too much time to do the whole lesson. The lesson itself addresses profound philosophical questions about causation.

Part I asks students to rank causes for war and how they got their assumptions about the causes of war. Part II introduces them to the concept that causes should be ranked, and that an interpretation really is an explanation of how the events led to war, that is, of why there was a war. The reading is by Thucydides, who is regarded as the father of modern history because of his views on causation. In Part III students have an opportunity to exercise their views on causation by examining a number of short interpretations on the causes of the Civil War. Part IV presents an "interpretation" which presents no explanation of how the events led to war.

Begin the lesson by having students individually fill in questions 1–3, then discuss question 4 in small groups. Have students individually answer questions 5 and 6, and then discuss in small groups again.

Parts II, III, and IV are set up to follow the same procedure. Students answer the questions individually, followed by small group discussion and then class discussion. Part III is rather lengthy, so it could be assigned as homework. The interpretations in Part III are short and don't contain detailed arguments or evidence. This is designed to focus student attention on general assumptions about the causes of war without dealing with other evaluation questions, such as evaluating evidence. Lesson 25 deals in more depth with four of the interpretations.

Suggested Answers
PART I

1. Question 1 forces students to think about the circumstance, if any, under which wars are justified. This question, along with questions 2 and 3 are meant to connect the Civil War with more recent wars, such as Vietnam and the Gulf War.

2. Question 2 is very important and will recur several

more times in the lesson. In general, historians look for underlying causes. You might want to point out that the word *interpretation* means to make understandable, to explain beyond the surface events, to explain why the events occurred the way they did. This question of specific events versus underlying causes is raised again in the Thucydides reading in Part II and in the interpretation in Part IV.

If students have difficulty understanding question 2, discuss it in terms of a familiar event, such as a fistfight. Paul took Leon's pen, Leon hit Paul and the two started fighting. Those are specific events. An underlying cause might be that Paul is always borrowing pens and forgetting to give them back. Or Leon is upset and angry about a home problem and lashed out at the first person who irritated him. Which explanation makes the causes of the fight clearer, the specific events or the underlying reasons?

3. Question 3 has students consider their own assumptions.

4. This leads to an interesting discussion in Question 4. Students may not have considered that assumptions about the world could influence the way one researches a topic and the selection of information to be included in an interpretation.

5. Question 5 prompts students to consider how they arrived at their own general assumptions.

6. Question 6 helps them connect their self-assessment to the backgrounds of historians. Factors in historians' backgrounds which might influence their views on wars are family background, such as a parent in the military or parents involved in peace movements; degree of intercultural contact, which would help a person see events from a variety of perspectives; travel; involvement in war; experiences and study in elementary and high school; college and graduate school attended; academic training; and home area.

PART II

7. Question 7—Thucydides would probably agree with a, c, and e. He would not have agreed with b. The idea that men do not control events, but are at the mercy of the gods, was Herodotus' view. Herodotus believed that the god Nemesis caused misfortune and failure to befall humans. Thucydides' analysis of human, political, and economic causes for events, and the

view that causes could be ranked in importance, are what make him the father of modern history in many people's opinion.

8. Student answers to Question 8 should raise some important philosophical questions related to the causes of the Civil War. Was the Civil War inevitable? At what point? Is there one main cause? Several main causes? Were men in control of events in the antebellum period?

PART III

9. Possible assumptions about the causes of war in the interpretations (students will choose two):

Interpretation	Assumptions
A	Poor leadership (abolitionist leaders) and slogans are important causes for war. The breakdown of politics and the willingness to fight for constitutional principles also leads to war. Secession inevitably leads to war.
B	A conspiracy which breaks the normal compromise of politics causes war. Attempts to get power cause war.
C	Moral issues are an important cause of wars. An important cause of war is the desire to stop a great evil.
D	Poor leadership and the breakdown of the compromise of politics causes wars. Individual leaders can cause wars.
E	Differences in culture cause wars.
F	The breakdown of the compromise of politics causes wars. Attempts to hold power cause war.
G	Economic conflict causes wars.
H	Same as D
I	Slogans and poor leadership are important causes of war. Wars are often unnecessary.
J	Same as C
K	Same as C
L	Political institutions (not necessarily the breakdown of compromise) cause wars.

10. The early interpretations emphasize the goodness of one side and the evil tendencies of the other side.

11. A reconsideration of whether the United States was justified in entering World War I and a general isolationist view of foreign policy in the 1930s may have influenced Interpretation I, which emphasizes war as a mistake. Interpretation J may have been influenced by the experience of fighting the clear evil of Nazi Germany.

12. Students should realize that events are always selected, consciously or subconsciously, based on the general assumptions the historians start with about the causes of war and based on the hypotheses they build about the particular war under study. Historians write with a particular frame of reference and select information to use in telling the story as they see it. How else could historians decide which information is important enough to include in their interpretations?

13. This question should generate an interesting discussion. One of my candidates for weakest is Interpretation D, which focuses the causes down to one person and one event. There is no explanation of how the violence of "bleeding Kansas" would lead to war years later. Violence = war is too simple. Have there been instances of violence when war was avoided?

14. Some trends students might note are

    • Historians have moved away from a good vs. evil perspective.

    • Historians now look at the causes as more complex than did earlier historians.

    • Historians are always using new methods, such as quantitative analysis of church attendance and voting.

PART IV

15. The explanation is not an interpretation. It doesn't really explain what caused the war. It just lists a bunch of events and assumes that the events themselves are the explanation for the Civil War. There is no effort to connect the events nor to explain the issues or forces which brought the events into play. Yet this is precisely how some textbooks read.

Lesson 25: What Were the Causes of the Civil War?

Objectives

To find the main idea
To recognize value claims and unstated assumptions
To evaluate evidence
To evaluate cause and effect
To evaluate comparisons
To evaluate generalizations
To evaluate debate reasoning
To evaluate proof by evidence

Teaching Ideas

Whereas Lesson 24 raises general philosophical questions about the causes of war and shows how those questions apply to very short summaries of many interpretations on the Civil War, this lesson presents four longer interpretations of the causes of the Civil War for analysis by students.

There are several ways to teach this lesson. You could have each student read all four interpretations and answer all the questions. Students in small groups could then discuss their answers, followed by discussion by the whole class. A second method is to group students and have each group evaluate one interpretation, either according to the questions in the lesson or according to the ARMEAR Model (p. 18 in the "Guide to Critical Thinking"). A third alternative is to have students read the four viewpoints, decide which viewpoint is strongest, and defend that position in a debate. Students could be required to do more research to prepare for the debate.

EXTENDING THE LESSON

No matter which strategy is chosen for the lesson, students could be assigned to research the causes further and write their own interpretation of the main causes of the Civil War. Students could be required to have a minimum amount of evidence (minimum number of endnotes) and to show why that evidence should be believed. They could also be required to defend their cause-and-effect arguments, generalizations, and so forth.

Suggested Answers
HISTORIAN A

These are suggested answers to the worksheet.

1. Main point—Slavery is the cause of the Civil War. Interestingly, this viewpoint violates a principle that many historians espouse—multiple causation. This idea that all events have several causes was men-

tioned in Lesson 24. Historian A commits the single cause fallacy (p. 6, "Guide to Critical Thinking"). At the end of the first paragraph, Historian A says that the Civil War would not have occurred without slavery. But that does not mean that slavery is the only cause. Just because a cause was necessary does not mean that it was sufficient to bring about an effect.

2. Cause and effect—Historian A shows a strong connection between slavery and secession, detailing how slavery led to increasing tensions. The connection between secession and the Civil War is nonexistent, dismissed in the final sentence, "The Civil War began soon after." Some might say secession made Civil War inevitable, but other historians disagree. Whole books have been written about the time period from secession to the outbreak of war. The connection needs to be shown.

   The historian also attempts, in the second paragraph, to eliminate another possible cause, the tariff dispute. Other causes, however, are not addressed.

3. In paragraph 4 Historian A says that *The Liberator* had small circulation, so may not have represented public opinion in the North. Then he asserts, without any support, that it nevertheless influenced many people in the North. This is a weak generalization. Paragraph 5 ends with an unsupported generalization that "many" Northerners were outraged.

4. Only three sources are offered to support Historian A's argument. The quote in paragraph 9 is by "Southerners" which isn't very specific. The statement in paragraph 8 is a primary source, but it doesn't mean very much—one person thought the war was inevitable. Senator Chase (paragraph 7) is a primary source, but is hardly objective, since he was upset by the Kansas-Nebraska Act. His statement does show that one Northerner was angry about slavery in the territories, but we don't know how well his statement represents Northern opinion in general.

5. Overall, the evidence is very weak. No evidence is offered to support the key points. Two pieces of evidence are opinions made by individuals.

6. This argument is weakened by the lack of evidence. It is also weak in one of the links in the cause-and-effect chain, as was explained in the answer to question 2.

HISTORIAN B

7. Main point—Economics is the main cause of the Civil War.

8. Cause and effect—Students should draw in the diagram like the one provided in question 2. Historian B presents arguments and information to show that economic issues caused problems between North and South, but not that the issues were important enough to cause a war. The various arguments show that some people were upset, but not that key leaders or most of the public were upset enough to fight. Also, like Historian A, this historian fails to connect secession to war (see answer to question 2). In paragraph 6, Historian B argues against slavery as a moral cause of the war. But he does not consider other possible causes, such as cultural differences or poor leadership.

9. Type of reasoning in paragraph 9—This is a generalization. We don't know what type of sample Historian B made. It is likely he looked at newspaper articles from the time. Do newspaper articles represent public opinion accurately?

10. Evaluate evidence—One source is quoted by Jefferson Davis in paragraph 5. He is a primary source about opinion at the time, but Davis has an obvious reason to lie to show that Northern opposition was self-serving rather than a principled attack on slavery. Davis surely doesn't want to focus attention on slavery.

11. Overall evaluation—This interpretation is even weaker than Historian A's argument, in that it does not show economics as a serious cause of secession let alone war. The evidence is also weak—there is no evidence to show that key people, or large numbers of people, were motivated by economics to break away or to fight.

HISTORIAN C

12. Main point—The North and South blundered into the Civil War. There was no sufficient cause.

13. Cause and effect—Again, many students will be helped by making the cause-and-effect diagram and filling it in (see question 2). Historian C does a good job of eliminating some of the popular causes for the Civil War (slavery and economics), but there may be other causes, such as differences in culture or the breakdown of political compromise, that should also be

considered. The connection between bogus leadership and war is really only argued in paragraph 7. Only three individuals are presented, and none of them is a key decision maker. If we had evidence that Lincoln, his cabinet, or Jefferson Davis, or his cabinet made emotional, irrational choices, or if we had evidence of widespread irrational behavior by the public, then we might see a better connection.

14. As mentioned above (answer 13), this is a very convincing argument against the spread of slavery as a cause of the Civil War. If people only thought there was a danger of slavery spreading, then they didn't have good enough reason to fight.

15. Footnotes 3 and 4 are important to the argument. Both are primary sources about emotional choices at the time. The quote by Douglas could have been taken out of context. At other points he may have been more optimistic—he may just have been discouraged at this one point. Toombs may also have been trying to discourage war to the person he was writing. Thus, he may have had a reason to lie. Emerson doesn't seem to have a reason to lie. Neither piece of evidence is very important since, as was mentioned in answer 13, they are both by individuals who were not decision makers. For all we know, everyone else in the country could have been perfectly rational, pushed into war by economics or slavery.

16. This interpretation is strong in eliminating two other popular causes of the war, but weak in establishing that poor leadership and fanaticism caused the war.

Historian D

17. Main point—The moral issue over slavery was the main cause of the Civil War.

18. Types of reasoning in paragraph 2—This is a comparison of the abolitionists to the anti-Nazis and the slaveholders to the Nazis. There are significant differences in the two cases. The abolitionists were not militarily invaded by the slaveholders as the anti-Nazis were. The slaveholders did not engage in genocide or threats to sovereign countries as the Nazis did. Therefore, while we might conclude that the anti-Nazis did the right thing in choosing to oppose the Nazis with force, we could still decide that the abolitionists did not make the right choice in their extreme opposition to slavery.

19. Historian D really does not show any connection between the moral question over slavery and war. No evidence is presented to show that a large number of Northerners were so upset by slavery that they wanted to fight to end it.

20. This is a weak argument, as explained in answers 18 and 19. Without evidence, it is difficult to accept the thesis.

GENERAL QUESTION

21. Students would have little idea about Historian B but might be able to take a reasonable guess about the other three interpretations. Historian A wrote at a time when moral issues such as impure meat and corruption were stressed by muckrakers. Historian B was a Progressive Historian, a school of history which emphasized economics as a prime force in events. Historian C wrote in the time period when Americans were fearful of being dragged into war in Europe, so reflected an isolationist perspective toward war. Historian D was obviously affected by the war against the Nazis.

Lesson 26: What Led to the Emancipation Proclamation and England's Neutrality in the Civil War?

Objectives

To relate relevant information to hypotheses
To assess cause and effect
To evaluate generalizations

Teaching Ideas

Have students read the theories and the relevant information and then answer questions 1–7 as instructed. You could tell students they don't have to fill in the answers to questions 1 to 6, which will save some time. But those questions force students to make more careful deliberations in deciding which theory is strongest. Cue students that some of the boxes in questions 1 and 6 should contain several of the relevant information letters.

Put students in small groups to discuss their answers, especially to questions 2 and 7. After discussing questions 1–7 or 2 and 7, have students answer question 8, then discuss it as a class. You can shorten the lesson by only discussing questions 2 and 7.

Suggested Answers
PART A—WHY DID
PRESIDENT LINCOLN ISSUE
THE EMANCIPATION
PROCLAMATION?

1. Strengths and weaknesses

   (See table next page.)

2. Theories C and D are best. D seems better than C because the bolstering of Northern morale seems important. Rather than debating with students, ask them to explain their answers. It is when they give their explanations that they will better learn how the various pieces of information fit together.

3. Theory C. Now the Battle of Antietam takes on greater significance. Emphasize that as new information is discovered, or utilized, interpretations change.

4. The information which is related to classes and class differences is K, R, and V; and information related to economics in A and O. You might want to discuss how a historian's frame of reference influences his/her interpretations of the past.

5. Possible answer:

   Political leaders often consider the international effects of internal policies. For example, President Lin-

Theory	Weaknesses	Strengths
A	G—shows that there weren't that many abolitionists, and that abolitionists would probably side with the North anyway.	J—raising morale seems to be important. D—changing the reason for fighting might reduce the high Southern morale.
B	How would the Emancipation Proclamation use industry to the fullest? B—shows that freeing the slaves wouldn't help keep the border states on the Northern side.	Same as strength for Theory A.
C	How would freeing the slaves capitalize on a Northern victory? The historian should show the connection better.	N, P, V—show that freeing the slaves might help keep England neutral.
D		Both of the reasons given make sense, as explained in the strengths for Theories A, B, and C.
E	Freeing the slaves as an act of strategy to help the Northern side would be done to try to neutralize all Southern advantages. Saying that it was to neutralize Southern military leaders doesn't explain anything.	Same as strength for Theory C.

coln was influenced in his decision to issue the Emancipation Proclamation by the effect of the policy on Europe. Lincoln freed the slaves partly to keep England and France neutral, since both countries would have found it difficult to support a society fighting to protect slavery.

PART B—WHY DIDN'T ENGLAND SIDE WITH THE SOUTH?

6. Strengths and weaknesses

   (See table top of next page.)

7. Theory A is better than B, C, or D because it includes the Emancipation Proclamation and explains why this cause is important.

8. Possible assessment:

   This generalization seems to apply very well to the case of England not siding with the South. Public opinion in England on the issue of slavery seems to have been a significant factor in the decision to not take sides in the Civil War.

Theory	Weaknesses	Strengths
A		Not wanting to side with a loser makes sense. F—shows North won. N, P, V—show that slavery was unpopular with many. C—shows unpopular wars are hard to fight.
B	K—shows monarchies usually oppose rebellions.	R—shows aristocrats sympathized with the South. Again, not wanting to side with a loser makes sense, and Northern industry is shown to be stronger (E).
C	How did the historian determine that England needed Northern wheat more than Southern cotton? The low Northern morale might as easily show why England would want to intervene (the South could win).	The low British unemployment rate may have slowed Britain from siding with the South. (Britain was doing fine without the war.)
D	A—shows England did need cotton, and information I shows England may have needed the cotton badly enough to build ships for the South (thereby antagonizing the North). Winning a battle might just as easily have brought England into the war (the South could win).	Same as strength for Theory A.

Lesson 27: What Role Did Racism Play in the Civil War and Nineteenth-Century America?

Objectives

To identify causes and effects
To evaluate sources
To identify unstated assumptions

Teaching Ideas

Begin by asking students if there is any harm in black icons, such as Aunt Jemima, or Sambo's Restaurant, or Little Black Sambo. Is there any harm in racial or ethnic jokes?

Instruct students to try their best to write an answer to question 1 (Sambo). Then go over it as a class so everyone has an idea of what to look for in the rest of Part I. Have students write answers to questions 2–6, discuss their answers in small groups, and go over them as a class.

In Part II, question 7 may be difficult for students. Go over Source A first, then have students do their best on the other sources. Have students in small groups discuss their answers to questions 7–11 and then discuss them as a whole class.

Suggested Answers
PART I

1. Sambo—This stereotype made blacks seem ideally suited to slavery, which took the responsibility of decision making away from the "childlike" slaves. It also showed that blacks were happy in slavery, since Sambo was always happy. An interesting question is how plantations could ever have been profitable if slaves were as lazy as the Sambo stereotype purported. The stereotype was an attempt to cover the brutality and inhumanity of slavery. It is likely that for whites in isolated parts of the North who had never seen a black, except for the portrayal of Sambo by white minstrels in blackface, the childlike image must have been a powerful stereotype.

2. Uncle Ned—The people who sang this song in the 1870s were looking back nostalgically on slavery, back to the time of the "happy darkie," who worked hard but also enjoyed himself with the fiddle. The "good darkie" is the obedient slave who in the end is rewarded. The message is we should go back to that tranquil time—slavery.

3. Zip Coon—By the 1860s and 1870s, when slavery had been abolished, this stereotype was popular in showing that blacks could not handle freedom. Blacks could try to imitate whites, but they'd look ridiculous because of their inferiority to whites. Zip Coon might use big words, but he wasn't smart enough to use them properly. Whites who saw minstrels playing Sambo and Zip Coon got two arguments in favor of slavery. Sambo was naturally suited to slavery, and Zip Coon could not handle emancipation.

4. The Savage—Another popular stereotype after the Civil War, the savage showed freedmen as a threat to white society. The wild nature of blacks again was a justification for slavery, but the savage stereotype also justified white lynchings of blacks. Some whites felt it necessary to kill blacks to protect white women from them.

5. Mammy—The mammy stereotype also showed slavery in a positive way. Mammy was devoted to her master's family. It was a tragedy to separate them. But mammy also covered over a very common problem in slavery—miscegenation. White owners raped slave women regularly. While historians disagree on the percentage of slave women who were abused, all agree it was a common practice. Two historians, Herbert Gutman and Richard Sutch, estimate that a slave woman had a 58% chance of being sexually abused by a white, mainly her owner, during the fifteen-year period of her youth. A planter in Louisiana told Frederick Law Olmstead in 1861, "There is not a likely-looking black girl in this state that is not the concubine of a white man...." The mammy stereotype avoided this problem simply through visual appearance. Mammy was fat and had her hair covered (hair is an important part of female sexual allure). She was a devoted worker, not someone who would be desired sexually. It wouldn't occur to white audiences viewing mammy that there had ever been a problem with miscegenation during slavery.

6. Picaninny—Picaninnies were wild, uncivilized, animal-like black children. But Picaninnies were victims, representing white desire that blacks would go away. ("Why don't they go back to Africa?") This desire to get rid of blacks is especially clear in the "Five Little Niggers" poem.

Part II

7. Causes of racism revealed in each source:

   A Simple solutions; fear; guilt

   B Insecurity, as revealed by fear of equality

   C Belief in the Sambo stereotype; ignorance

   D Belief in the Sambo stereotype; ignorance

   E Blaming the victims. The war is blamed on blacks for being slaves, it seems.

   G Economic competition for jobs; blaming blacks for the war

   H Political opportunism—since whites could vote and blacks could not, the political appeal is addressed to whites, appealing to their racism

8. As noted above, Abraham Lincoln (source C) and whites in the north (source D) may have been influenced by the Sambo as well as the Zip Coon stereotypes. Blacks were incapable of responsible independent action, according to the stereotype and these sources.

9. There are a number of possible causes for the change in attitude:

   • Leadership in Washington had set a new direction, so many ordinary people changed their position. It was war, after all, so to disagree with official policy might be seen as undermining the war effort.

   • People saw articles in the newspapers favoring black soldiers.

   • Blacks who had fought did so heroically, so people may have changed their views of the capabilities of blacks.

   • Some people may have felt that blacks were necessary to win the war.

   • The change was happening whether whites liked it or not, so why fight it?

   • More blacks fighting meant fewer white casualties.

10. Among the problems blacks face:

   • Racial jokes and insults by whites in the Union army

- Death sentence by Confederate army on black Union soldiers captured

- Lack of the best equipment, especially shoes

- Lower pay than whites

- Black soldiers being led by white officers

- Segregated regiments

11. Evaluate the sources:

- All are primary sources in revealing a particular attitude by whites about blacks, except possibly Source D, which makes claims about most observing and thoughtful people without having a direct observation of that attitude toward blacks.

- Sources A, E, and F are private, so have no obvious reason to lie.

- Sources B, C, and H don't have an obvious reason to lie, since they are "innocent" documents. That is, they were written for some other purpose, but unwittingly reveal racism.

- Sources D and G are public and have a desire to prove a particular point of view, so they must be used with more caution.

- All the sources support the same conclusion that many whites in the North had racist attitudes toward blacks in the Civil War. That is, each source has other sources supporting its point of view.

PART I—INDIVIDUAL SKILLS

Identifying Evidence

Q Label each item below with the appropriate letter.

    S   A **source** of information is given.

    N   **No** source of information is given.

_____ 1. The Ken Burns series of films on the Civil War showed that during the war, many men missed their wives terribly.

_____ 2. A sketch by T. R. Davis of a slave auction highlights the inhumanity of slavery.

_____ 3. Slavery was much worse in the United States than it was in other countries in the Western Hemisphere.

_____ 4. Many women were interested in getting rights in the mid-1800s, as shown in the Seneca Falls Declaration.

_____ 5. More Americans were lost at the Battle of Gettysburg than in the entire American Revolution.

Evaluating Evidence

Q In the space provided, use at least three of the criteria you learned in class to evaluate the following evidence.

A. Ilana Frost, candidate for Congress in the 6th District, charged her opponent with taking bribes from a construction company two years ago.

  6. Strengths:

  7. Weaknesses:

[Continued on next page.]

©1993 Critical Thinking Press & Software, P.O. Box 448, Pacific Grove, CA 93950 (800) 458-4849

[Continued from previous page.]

B. We want to know if some abolitionists were radical and uncompromising in their views on slavery. The abolitionist William Lloyd Garrison said in a newspaper article in 1831, "I will be as harsh as truth and as uncompromising as justice. On this subject [of slavery], I do not wish to think, to speak, or write in moderation. No! No!...I will not excuse—I will not retreat a single inch...."

   8. Strengths:

   9. Weaknesses:

C. Congressman Felix Grundy of Tennessee said in a speech to Congress on December 9, 1811, "In the West, it is with British help and encouragement that the Indians have begun to fight us." He then called for Congress to take action against Britain.

  10. Strengths:

  11. Weaknesses:

D. President James Madison said in his message to Congress on June 1, 1812, that Congress should declare war on Britain because British ships continued to violate the rights of Americans on the seas and because the British were arming the Indians who in turn were attacking Americans on the frontier.

  12. Strengths:

[Continued on next page.]

[Continued from previous page.]

13. Weaknesses:

E. The slave Henry Bibb wrote a letter in March 1844 to his former owner in which he recounted how the owner had whipped and slashed his wife "without mercy."

14. Strengths:

15. Weaknesses:

F. Former slave Henry Baker was interviewed in 1938 at the age of 83. He stated that slaves had been whipped regularly on the plantation where he was a slave.

16. Strengths:

17. Weaknesses:

[Continued on next page.]

[Continued from previous page.]

Identifying Cause-and-Effect Reasoning

Q Label each item below with the appropriate letter.

> **C-E** The item involves **cause-and-effect** reasoning.
>
> **N** The item does **not** involve cause-and-effect reasoning.

_____18. American manufacturing grew tremendously due to the War of 1812.

_____19. The price of cotton dropped in the 1850s.

_____20. Andrew Jackson was one of our most active presidents in the 1800s.

_____21. People reacted to the evils of slavery by trying to abolish it.

Evaluating Cause-and-Effect Reasoning

Q Evaluate the following cause-and-effect arguments by filling in the boxes and answering the questions.

22. The fanatical actions of the abolitionists led to the Civil War. The statement by the famous abolitionist Henry Garret that slaves should rise up against their owners shows this fanaticism. He specifically said, "Rather die like free men than live like slaves." When people talked like this, there was no chance for compromise, and the Civil War could not be prevented.

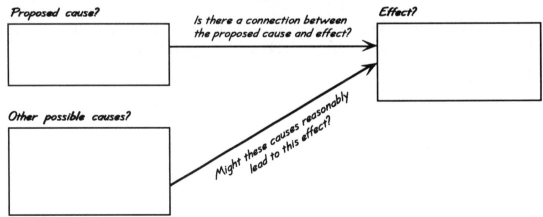

Overall, how strong is this reasoning?

[Continued on next page.]

[Continued from previous page.]

23. The Embargo Act and the War of 1812 led to the industrial revolution in the United States. The Embargo Act cut off trade with England, then the war prevented the United States from getting products from Europe. Consequently, Americans began to make many of the products themselves.

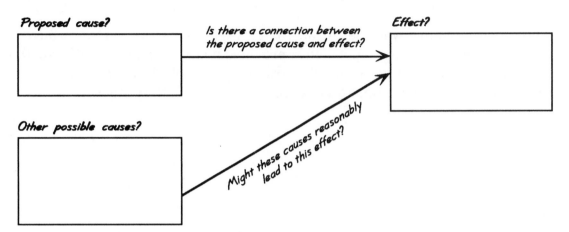

Overall, how strong is this reasoning?

Identifying Comparisons

Q Label each item below with the appropriate letter.

> **C** The item involves **comparison** reasoning.
>
> **N** The item does **not** involve comparison reasoning.

_____ 24. The Seneca Falls Declaration was an important step in securing rights for women.

_____ 25. Andrew Jackson was the John F. Kennedy of the 1830s. He was an active president who took a strong stand for the people.

_____ 26. Cotton producers were worse off in 1860 than they were in 1850. Prices had dropped, which reduced profits.

[Continued on next page.]

[Continued from previous page.]

Evaluating Comparisons

 Evaluate the following comparison arguments. Explain whether the comparison is strong or weak and why you think so.

27. Slaves in the South were better off than "wage slaves" in Northern factories. Slaves had food, clothing, and shelter provided by their masters while Northern factory workers were guaranteed nothing. Wages of Northern workers were often too low to survive on, and if workers were fired, they starved.

28. The Civil War was far more horrible than the American Revolution. The casualties in just one big battle, such as Antietem or Gettysburg, exceeded American casualties in the entire Revolution.

Identifying Generalizations

 Label each of the following with the appropriate letter.

G   The item involves **generalization** reasoning.

N   The item does **not** involve generalization reasoning.

_____29.   Canals improved the transportation of goods in the United States.

_____30.   Robert E. Lee was a great general in the Civil War.

_____31.   There were few slave revolts in the United States.

_____32.   The U.S. Bank recharter was vetoed by President Jackson.

[Continued on next page.]

[Continued from previous page.]

Evaluating Generalizations

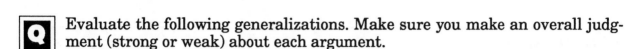 Evaluate the following generalizations. Make sure you make an overall judgment (strong or weak) about each argument.

33. Very few Northerners voted for the Liberty (anti-slavery) Party in the 1844 election, which shows how little support the abolitionists actually had.

34. Articles written in magazines making fun of the Seneca Falls Convention show that most men did not take women's rights seriously.

Identifying Types of Reasoning

Identify the type of reasoning in each of the following by writing the letter of the correct answer.

        A—Comparison

        B—Generalization

        C—Cause and effect

        D—Proof by Authority

_____35. Lincoln's election in 1860 scared the South to death. With slavery threatened, Southern states felt they had no other choice but to secede (break away) from the Union.

_____36. Slaves were fed an adequate diet in terms of calories but not in terms of nutrients.

_____37. The Mexican government refused to see the United States Ambassador, which was a big factor in bringing about the Mexican War.

_____38. The South lost the Civil War primarily because the North had a larger population and factory base.

_____39. Bruce Catton, in his prize-winning book on the Civil War, says that the South came close to victory in 1862.

_____40. In terms of working conditions, industrialization was not as bad in the United States as in England.

_____41. Most women were not active in politics in the early 1800s.

[Continued on next page.]

[Continued from previous page.]

PART II—MIXED PROBLEMS

Historian Y

(1) Slaves in the United States generally ate a large amount of food which provided sufficient energy to work hard, but which did not provide a balanced diet. Slaves thus suffered from a number of dietary deficiencies and nutritional diseases. There were several reasons for this poor nutritional diet.

(2) A minority (less than 50%) of masters didn't even supply their slaves with enough food. These owners were trying to cut costs by buying less food. A person from North Carolina complained in 1853, "There are many farmers who feed their negroes sparingly, believing that it is economy, that they save by it, but such is not the fact."[1] Sometimes owners were short of cash and could not buy as much food, which led to less food for slaves.

(3) A second reason for the poor slave diet was poor food preparation (cooking, etc.) on many plantations. Many owners left the preparation of food to the slaves, but the slaves did not have enough time to cook the food well. One plantation owner explained, "The cooking being done [by slaves] in a hurry, is badly done; being usually burnt on the outside while it is still raw within and consequently unhealthy."[2]

(4) The most important reason, however, for the poor slave diet was the lack of knowledge on the part of owners about nutrition. No one in the 19th century knew much about the science of dietetics, and this included slave owners. An essay published in 1859 by Dr. John Wilson on the feeding of Negroes illustrates the ignorance of even the medical profession of nutrition principles. Dr. Wilson divided all foods into two categories: "nitrogenized or muscle-producing and non-nitrogenized or heat producing." He said that the fatty, heat-producing foods (such as corn and pork) "generate sufficient heat to cause the wheels of life to move glibly and smoothly, and hence negroes who are freely supplied with them grow plump, sleek, and shiny."[3] Most owners simply never realized that it might be necessary to feed their slaves anything other than corn and pork. This lack of knowledge of nutrition is also shown in that even owners and their families rarely had a balanced diet.

(5) With the amount of food sometimes supplied by stingy owners, the inadequate (poor) preparation of the food, and the lack of knowledge of nutrition by owners, slaves ate a poor nutritional diet.

Endnotes for Historian Y

1. *Farmer's Journal*, II (1853), p. 53.
2. *De Bow's Review*, XIII (1852), pp. 193–94.
3. *American Cotton Planter and Soil of the South*, III (1859), p. 197.

[Continued on next page.]

[Continued from previous page.]

 Questions

_____42. What is the main point of Historian Y?

 A. Dr. John Wilson had a poor understanding of nutrition.

 B. Poor food preparation led to a poor nutritional diet for slaves.

 C. Slaves generally received sufficient energy from their food, but had a poor nutritional diet.

 D. Slave owners sometimes tried to save money by feeding their slaves less food.

43. Evaluate one piece of evidence in Historian Y's argument.

44. What type of reasoning is used in the first sentence of paragraph 4?

45. Evaluate the reasoning from #44.

46. What type of reasoning is used in the first sentence of paragraph 2?

47. Evaluate the reasoning from #46.

[Continued on next page.]

[Continued from previous page.]

Suppose there are three historians with the following views of the main cause of the Civil War:

Historian A

The moral issue of slavery was the main cause of the Civil War.

Historian B

Economic differences between the North and South were the main cause of the Civil War.

Historian C

There was no adequate cause for the Civil War. Poor political leadership in the 1850s pushed the country into a needless war.

 Show how each of the following pieces of information affects the above three theories:

_____48. New England (Northern) textile mills depended upon Southern cotton. If the cotton system were disrupted by war, the textile mills would be hurt badly and many would go out of business. This evidence <u>most directly</u>

    A. Weakens Historian A's argument

    B. Weakens Historian B's argument

    C. Weakens Historian C's argument

    D. Supports Historian A's argument

    E. Supports Historian B's argument

_____49. Statement by William Lloyd Garrison in a newspaper article in 1831: "I will be as harsh as truth and as uncompromising as justice. On this subject [of slavery], I do not wish to think, to speak, or write in moderation. No! No!...I will not excuse—I will not retreat a single inch...."

    A. Weakens Historian A

    B. Weakens Historian B

    C. Weakens Historian C

    D. Supports Historian A

    E. Supports Historian B

[Continued on next page.]

[Continued from previous page.]

_____ 50. Henry Garnet, a radical abolitionist, said in 1843, "Brethren, Arise, Arise! Let every slave throughout the land do this, and the days of slavery are numbered. Rather die like free men than live like slaves."

A. Weakens Historian A

B. Weakens Historian B

C. Supports Historian C

D. Supports Historian A

E. Supports Historian B

TEST QUESTION ANSWERS

Teaching Ideas

As mentioned in the introduction, students should be evaluated in a variety of ways, not just by objective tests. So although fifty test items are included in the *Teacher's Guide*, you should also consider evaluating students using problems from the student text. One of the best evaluation methods is to give students an interpretation you haven't analyzed in class and have them write an evaluation of it. You could supply the criteria for evaluation, such as finding the main idea, identifying and evaluating two pieces of evidence, identifying and evaluating two types of reasoning, identifying one assumption, bringing in any relevant information on the topic, and making an overall judgment.

The fifty items on the test are meant to examine student mastery of the skills listed on the scope and sequence chart on pages 12–13, primarily identifying and evaluating evidence, cause-and-effect reasoning, comparison reasoning, and generalization reasoning.

Suggested Answers

IDENTIFYING EVIDENCE

Part I Individual skills

1. S The Ken Burns series is the source.

2. S The sketch is the source.

3. N

4. S The Seneca Falls Declaration is the source.

5. N

EVALUATING EVIDENCE

A. Frost

6. Strengths: None

7. Weaknesses: Secondary source; reason to lie; no other evidence; public statement

B. Garrison

8. Strengths: Primary source; probably no reason to lie about being unreasonable

9. Weaknesses: No other evidence; public statement; maybe he's talking radical in public but would compromise in private

C. Grundy

   10. Strengths: None

   11. Weaknesses: Secondary source; no other evidence; reason to lie; public statement

D. Madison

   12. Strengths: None

   13. Weaknesses: Secondary source; no other evidence; reason to lie; public statement

E. Bibb

   14. Strengths: Primary source; private letter

   15. Weaknesses: Possibly has a reason to lie; no other evidence

F. Baker

   16. Strengths: Primary source

   17. Weaknesses: Reason to lie; no other evidence; public statement; taken many years after the event (could forget a lot)

IDENTIFYING CAUSE-AND-EFFECT REASONING

18. C-E

19. N

20. N

21. C-E

EVALUATING CAUSE-AND-EFFECT REASONING

22. Abolitionists

Proposed Cause: Fanatical actions of abolitionists

Connection: It is reasonable that fanatical action might lead to hard feelings and maybe an unwillingness to compromise. But that would not necessarily lead to war. Many fanatical proposals have been made that did not end in war. Besides, this author did not show that the fanatical actions led to hard feelings or unwillingness to compromise. A clear connection was not shown.

Stated Effect: Civil War

Other possible causes for Civil War: Economic problems; poor leadership; political struggle over power in Congress; specific crises (John Brown's raid, Bleeding Kansas)

Overall: This is a very weak argument. This may *be* a cause, but it is not *the* cause of the Civil War (single cause fallacy, p. 6). The connection was not made, and other causes seem as likely as the proposed cause.

23. Embargo Act

Proposed Cause: Embargo Act and War of 1812

Connection: It makes sense that a restriction of imports might lead to industrial production to obtain the goods. However, it could also have led to opening trade with other areas of the world.

Stated Effect: Industrial revolution in the United States

Other possible causes for the industrial revolution in the United States: Technological breakthroughs, inventions, labor shortage, large quantity of capital available for investment in machines

Overall: It is reasonable that the Embargo and War would lead to production of more goods within the United States but not necessarily to *industrial* production. There must have been other factors involved.

IDENTIFYING COMPARISONS

24. N

25. C

26. C   "Worse off" compares 1850 to 1860.

EVALUATING COMPARISONS

27. Slaves may have had better material possessions than those who had no income or no job. But slaves had no freedom—an important difference. Free men had the potential to accumulate much better homes, clothing, and food, while slaves did not. This comparison omits an important difference.

28. Both were wars, and both were fought in the United States. Different reasons for the casualties don't matter, since the argument does not make claims about why the casualties were different. One significant difference is the casualties of both sides were counted in the Civil War since both sides were Americans. This doubling of casualties does not account for the tremendous increase, however, where there were as many killed and wounded in one battle as there were in the entire Revolution. The comparison is reasonable.

IDENTIFYING GENERALIZATIONS

29. G   "Canals"—plural noun

30. N

31. G   "Few" and "revolts"

32. N

EVALUATING GENERALIZATIONS

33. In terms of voters, this is a good sample (100%). However, people who supported the abolitionists may not have voted for the Liberty Party because they didn't want to waste their vote on a third party. Moreover, abolitionist support may have been much stronger among the nonvoting part of the population. Overall, this is a fairly weak generalization.

34. The articles tell us very little about the views of men in general. It merely shows the views of writers of magazine articles. This is a weak generalization, much weaker than the one in #33.

IDENTIFYING TYPES OF REASONING

35. C; also a generalization (B)

36. B

37. C

38. C

39. D

40. A

41. B

Part II Mixed Problems

HISTORIAN Y

42. C

43. Evaluate one piece of evidence

Quote, 2nd paragraph (endnote 1)—This source is contemporary and would be considered by most people to be a primary source; there is no obvious reason to lie; it is public; there are no other sources supporting this claim.

44. Reasoning, first sentence of paragraph 4

This is mainly cause and effect; also generalization.

45. Evaluate reasoning

There is a clear connection between lack of nutrition knowledge and poor nutrition. However, owners also may have been feeding slaves corn and pork because it was cheaper.

46. Reasoning, first sentence of paragraph 2
    Generalization

47. Evaluate reasoning
    The evidence from one journal article provides some support, but we need more examples to show the practice of providing inadequate food quantities was widespread. We need a larger, more representative sample.

HISTORIAN A, B, C

48. B

49. D

50. D